taste of home
Southern
FAVORITES

49

52

60

89

taste of home
Southern
FAVORITES

VICE PRESIDENT, EDITOR-IN-CHIEF:	Catherine Cassidy
VICE PRESIDENT, EXECUTIVE EDITOR/BOOKS:	Heidi Reuter Lloyd
CREATIVE DIRECTOR:	Howard Greenberg
FOOD DIRECTOR:	Diane Werner, RD
SENIOR EDITOR/BOOKS:	Mark Hagen
EDITORS:	Amy Glander, Krista Lanphier
ASSOCIATE CREATIVE DIRECTOR:	Edwin Robles Jr.
ART DIRECTOR:	Jessie Sharon
CONTENT PRODUCTION MANAGER:	Julie Wagner
LAYOUT DESIGNER:	Kathy Crawford
COPY CHIEF:	Deb Warlaumont Mulvey
COPY EDITOR:	Susan Uphill
RECIPE ASSET SYSTEM MANAGER:	Coleen Martin
RECIPE TESTING AND EDITING:	Taste of Home Test Kitchen
FOOD PHOTOGRAPHY:	Taste of Home Photo Studio
COVER PHOTOGRAPHER:	Rob Hagen
COVER FOOD STYLIST:	Veronica Day
COVER SET STYLIST:	Deone Jahnke
ADMINISTRATIVE ASSISTANT:	Barb Czysz

NORTH AMERICAN CHIEF MARKETING OFFICER:	Lisa Karpinski
VICE PRESIDENT/BOOK MARKETING:	Dan Fink
CREATIVE DIRECTOR/CREATIVE MARKETING:	Jim Palmen

The Reader's Digest Association, Inc.

PRESIDENT AND CHIEF EXECUTIVE OFFICER:	Tom Williams
EXECUTIVE VICE PRESIDENT, RDA, AND PRESIDENT, NORTH AMERICA:	Dan Lagani

Front cover, counterclockwise from top: Strawberry Rhubarb Pie (p. 92), Country Fried Chicken (p. 71), Creamy Succotash (p. 50), Southern Buttermilk Biscuits (p. 25), Sweet Tea Concentrate (p. 7).

Back cover, top to bottom: Avocado Shrimp Salsa (p. 14), Ham 'n' Corn Fritters (p. 17), Vegetable Beef Soup (p. 28), Black-Eyed Pea Salad (p. 37), Pineapple Upside-Down Cake (p. 91), Barbecued Sticky Ribs (p. 61).

International Standard Book Number (10): 0-89821-951-5
International Standard Book Number (13): 978-0-89821-951-7
Library of Congress Control Number: 2011931582

Printed in China.

For other Taste of Home books and products, visit ShopTasteofHome.com

table of contents

45

17

74

73

47

Southern cooking done right!

Southerners have always had a love affair with food. And as any self-respecting Southern family cook can attest, this unbridled affection is rooted in warm hospitality, down-home comfort and, most importantly, the use of just-ripe, fresh-from-the-farm ingredients.

But you don't need to live south of the Mason-Dixon Line to savor the tantalizing flavors and mouthwatering combinations that have made Southern cuisine so famous. With *Taste of Home Southern Favorites* in hand, you can enjoy nearly 200 richly satisfying Southern specialties right in the comfort of your kitchen, no matter what neck of the woods you happen to call home.

This downright delicious cookbook features all the classics...chicken fried to perfection, fork-tender beef brisket, saucy barbecued ribs, fiery jambalayas, satisfying sides, golden baked breads and biscuits, heavenly desserts and a host of other stick-to-your-ribs favorites.

Planning a backyard get-together? Guests will go hog wild for succulent Slow-Cooked Pork Barbecue (p. 37) smothered in a tangy sauce and served alongside a helping of Sweet 'n' Sour Coleslaw (p. 38).

Looking to fire up the flavor of dinner tonight? Try Creole Jambalaya (p. 34) or Crawfish Etouffee (p. 28) for a little heat. Find cool relief with a refreshing side of Watermelon and Tomato Salad (p. 45) or a tall glass of Raspberry Sweet Tea (p. 10).

When casual comfort food is in order, sink your teeth into Shrimp Po' Boys (p. 43) or Italian Muffuletta (p. 45). For a hot and steamy pot of goodness, slowly savor hearty spoonfuls of Crab Corn Chowder (p. 35), or any of the soups, stews or chili found here.

Need to round out the meal? You can't go wrong with our selection of heartwarming side dishes, salads, appetizers and breads. Creamy Succotash (p. 50), Buttermilk Corn Bread (p. 19) and Cheese 'n' Grits Casserole (p. 47) are just a sampling of the many accompaniments that turn a ho-hum meal into something spectacular.

We even have a hearty selection of breakfast and brunch recipes that start the day off right! Wake up your taste buds with Benedict Eggs in Pastry (p. 73), New Orleans Beignets (p. 78) and other rise-and-shine delights.

And if your meal just isn't complete without dessert, indulge your fancy with Bananas Foster (p. 105), Lemon-Filled Coconut Cake (p. 90) or Peach Blackberry Cobbler (p. 101). They end any meal on a sweet note.

So grab your cast-iron skillet and get ready to dig into a bounty of dishes that turn out slick as butter every time. With culinary creations hailing from the bayous of Louisiana, the low country of the Carolinas, the deep heart of Texas and even the renowned eateries of New Orleans, each authentic gem of a recipe inside *Southern Favorites* celebrates the South in all its lip-smackin', finger-lickin' glory!

67

7

44

63

great gift!

Southern Favorites makes a great gift for those who are passionate about Southern food. To order additional copies, specify item number 42100 and send $14.99 (plus $4.99 shipping/processing for one book, $5.99 for two or more) to:

Shop Taste of Home, Suite 515
P.O. Box 26820
Lehigh Valley, PA 18002-6280.

To order by credit card,
call toll-free 800/880-3012.

42

47

33

92

9   10   12   15

WATERMELON SALSA

appetizers & beverages

watermelon salsa

PREP: 20 min. + chilling | **YIELD:** 3 cups.

I entered my salsa recipe in a local contest and won first place! It was a special honor because all of the ingredients—except for the lime juice—came directly from my own garden and bee hives.
CAROLYN BUTTERFIELD, LAKE STEVENS, WASHINGTON

  2 cups seeded finely chopped watermelon
 1/2 cup finely chopped peeled cucumber
 1/4 cup finely chopped red onion
 1/4 cup finely chopped sweet red pepper
  1 jalapeno pepper, seeded and minced
 1/4 cup minced fresh cilantro
  1 tablespoon minced fresh basil
  1 tablespoon minced fresh mint
  2 tablespoons honey
  1 teaspoon lime juice
Baked tortilla chip scoops

In a large bowl, combine the watermelon, cucumber, onion, peppers and herbs. Drizzle with honey and lime juice; gently toss to coat.

Refrigerate for at least 1 hour. Serve with chips.

EDITOR'S NOTE: We recommend wearing disposable gloves when cutting hot peppers. Avoid touching your face.

sweet tea concentrate

PREP: 30 min. + cooling
YIELD: 20 servings (5 cups concentrate).

This refreshingly sweet cooler is a Southern classic. Whip up a batch to serve at your next party or picnic or make a single glass to sip slowly on a hot, sticky day.
NATALIE BREMSON, PLANTATION, FLORIDA

   2   medium lemons
   4   cups sugar
   4   cups water
 1-1/2 cups English breakfast tea leaves *or*
       20 black tea bags
  1/3 cup lemon juice
EACH SERVING:
   1   cup cold water
Ice cubes

Remove peels from lemons; save fruit for another use.

In a large saucepan, combine sugar and water. Bring to a boil over medium heat. Reduce heat; simmer, uncovered, for 3-5 minutes or until sugar is dissolved, stirring occasionally. Remove from heat; add tea leaves and lemon peels. Cover and steep for 15 minutes. Strain tea, discarding tea leaves and lemon peels; stir in lemon juice. Cool to room temperature.

Transfer to a container with a tight-fitting lid. Store in the refrigerator for up to 2 weeks.

TO PREPARE TEA: In a tall glass, combine water with 1/4 cup concentrate; add ice.

cream cheese deviled eggs

PREP/TOTAL TIME: 25 min. | **YIELD:** 16 appetizers.

Peas and bacon give this traditional appetizer a fun twist. A family favorite, these deviled eggs are always first to disappear from the buffet table.
ABI MCMAHON, SHERMAN OAKS, CALIFORNIA

  8 hard-cooked eggs
  1 package (8 ounces) cream cheese, softened
  2 teaspoons Dijon mustard
 1/4 teaspoon salt
 1/4 teaspoon pepper
 1/4 cup frozen peas, thawed
  3 bacon strips, cooked and crumbled

Cut eggs in half lengthwise. Remove yolks; set whites aside. In a small bowl, mash yolks. Add the cream cheese, mustard, salt and pepper; beat until blended. Stir in peas.

Stuff or pipe mixture into egg whites. Sprinkle with bacon. Refrigerate until serving.

cream cheese deviled eggs

homemade lemonade

coconut fried shrimp

PREP/TOTAL TIME: 20 min. | **YIELD:** 4 servings.

These crunchy shrimp make a tempting appetizer or a fun change-of-pace main entree. The coconut coating adds a little sweetness, and the tangy orange marmalade and honey sauce is great for dipping. It's impossible to stop munching these once you start!

ANN ATCHISON, O'FALLON, MISSOURI

1-1/4	cups all-purpose flour
1-1/4	cups cornstarch
6-1/2	teaspoons baking powder
1/2	teaspoon salt
1/4	teaspoon Cajun seasoning
1-1/2	cups cold water
1/2	teaspoon canola oil
2-1/2	cups flaked coconut
1	pound uncooked large shrimp, peeled and deveined
Additional oil for deep-fat frying	
1	cup orange marmalade
1/4	cup honey

In a large bowl, combine the first five ingredients. Stir in water and oil until smooth. Place coconut in another bowl. Dip shrimp into batter, then coat with coconut.

In an electric skillet or deep-fat fryer, heat oil to 375°. Fry shrimp, a few at a time, for 3 minutes or until golden brown. Drain on paper towels.

In a small saucepan, heat marmalade and honey; stir until blended. Serve with shrimp.

TEST KITCHEN TIP: Do not fry more than two to three shrimp at a time or the temperature of the oil will lower and the shrimp will not be crisp.

homemade lemonade

PREP: 5 min. | **COOK:** 10 min. + chilling | **YIELD:** 10 cups.

There's no better way to cool down on a hot day than with an ice-cold glass of my old-fashioned lemonade. Club soda adds a refreshing fizz.

REBECCA BAIRD, SALT LAKE CITY, UTAH

3	cups sugar
2	cups water
1	cup lemon peel strips (about 6 lemons)
3	cups lemon juice (about 14 lemons)
1	bottle (1 liter) club soda, chilled

In a large saucepan, heat sugar and water over medium heat until sugar is dissolved, stirring frequently. Stir in the lemon strips. Bring to a boil. Reduce heat; simmer, uncovered, for 5 minutes. Remove from the heat. Cool slightly. Stir in lemon juice; cover and refrigerate until chilled. Discard lemon strips. Pour mixture into a pitcher; gradually stir in club soda.

ORANGE LEMONADE: Heat 1-3/4 cups sugar with 2-1/2 cups water as directed. Cool sugar syrup. Add 1-1/2 cups each lemon and orange juices, and 2 tablespoons each grated lemon and orange peels. Strain lemonade mixture and refrigerate until chilled. For each serving, fill a glass with 1/2 cup of lemonade mixture and 1/2 cup of chilled water or club soda. Add ice and serve.

coconut fried shrimp

crab cakes with red chili mayo

PREP: 35 min. + chilling | **COOK:** 10 min./batch
YIELD: 2 dozen (1 cup sauce).

This is one of my most popular appetizers. The spicy mayo is just the right accent for the crab cakes.
TIFFANY ANDERSON-TAYLOR, GULFPORT, FLORIDA

1-1/3	cups mayonnaise
2	tablespoons Thai chili sauce
2	teaspoons lemon juice, *divided*
1/4	cup *each* finely chopped celery, red onion and sweet red pepper
1	jalapeno pepper, seeded and finely chopped
4	tablespoons olive oil, *divided*
1/2	cup soft bread crumbs
1	egg, lightly beaten
1	pound fresh crabmeat
1/4	cup all-purpose flour

In a small bowl, combine the mayonnaise, chili sauce and 1-1/4 teaspoons lemon juice. Set aside.

In a small skillet, saute the celery, onion, red pepper and jalapeno in 1 tablespoon oil until tender. Transfer to a large bowl; stir in the bread crumbs, egg, 1/2 cup reserved mayonnaise mixture and remaining lemon juice. Fold in crab. Cover and refrigerate for at least 2 hours. Cover and refrigerate remaining mayonnaise mixture for sauce.

Place flour in a shallow bowl. Drop crab mixture by 2 tablespoonfuls into flour. Gently coat and shape into a 1/2-in.-thick patty. Repeat with remaining mixture.

In a large skillet over medium-high heat, cook patties in remaining oil in batches for 3-4 minutes on each side or until golden brown. Serve with reserved sauce.

EDITOR'S NOTE: We recommend wearing disposable gloves when cutting hot peppers. Avoid touching your face.

raspberry sweet tea

PREP: 20 min. + chilling | **YIELD:** 15 servings.

You only need a handful of ingredients to stir together this sweet tea. Its vibrant color and smile-fetching flavor make it a popular thirst quencher in warm weather.
TASTE OF HOME TEST KITCHEN

4	**quarts water,** *divided*
1	**cup sugar**
10	**individual tea bags**
1	**package (12 ounces) frozen unsweetened raspberries, thawed and undrained**
3	**tablespoons lime juice**

In a large saucepan, bring 2 qts. of water to a boil. Stir in sugar until dissolved. Remove from the heat.

Add tea bags; steep for 5-8 minutes. Discard tea bags.

In another saucepan, bring raspberries and remaining water to a boil. Reduce heat; simmer, uncovered, for 3 minutes. Strain and discard pulp. Add raspberry and lime juices to the tea.

Transfer to a large pitcher. Refrigerate until chilled.

raspberry sweet tea

candied pecans

candied pecans

PREP: 20 min. | **BAKE:** 40 min. | **YIELD:** about 1 pound.

Candied pecans are considered an iconic sweet in the South. I pack these crispy sugared delights in jars tied with pretty ribbons for family and friends.
OPAL TURNER, HUGHES SPRINGS, TEXAS

2-3/4	**cups pecan halves**
2	**tablespoons butter, softened,** *divided*
1	**cup sugar**
1/2	**cup water**
1/2	**teaspoon salt**
1/2	**teaspoon ground cinnamon**
1	**teaspoon vanilla extract**

Place pecans in a shallow baking pan in a 250° oven for 10 minutes or until warmed. Grease a 15-in. x 10-in. x 1-in. baking pan with 1 tablespoon butter; set aside.

Grease the sides of a large heavy saucepan with remaining butter; add sugar, water, salt and cinnamon. Cook and stir over low heat until sugar is dissolved. Cook and stir over medium heat until mixture comes to a boil. Cover and cook for 2 minutes to dissolve sugar crystals.

Cook, without stirring, until a candy thermometer reads 236° (soft-ball stage). Remove from the heat; add vanilla. Stir in warm pecans until evenly coated.

Spread onto prepared baking pan. Bake at 250° for 30 minutes, stirring every 10 minutes. Spread on a waxed paper-lined baking sheet to cool.

EDITOR'S NOTE: We recommend that you test your candy thermometer before each use by bringing water to a boil; the thermometer should read 212°. Adjust your recipe temperature up or down based on your test.

benedictine dip

PREP/TOTAL TIME: 15 min. | **YIELD:** 1-3/4 cups.

Benedictine is a creamy spread studded with chopped cucumbers. It was named after Jennie Carter Benedict, a chef and restaurateur from Louisville, Kentucky, who created the condiment at the turn of the 20th century. Originally used for cucumber sandwiches, Benedictine is now commonly enjoyed as a cold dip for chips or spread on crackers.
TASTE OF HOME TEST KITCHEN

4	ounces cream cheese, softened
1	log (4 ounces) fresh goat cheese
2	tablespoons minced fresh parsley
1	tablespoon mayonnaise
1/4	teaspoon salt
1/8	teaspoon cayenne pepper
1/8	teaspoon pepper
1	drop green food coloring, optional
3/4	cup finely chopped peeled cucumber, patted dry
1/4	cup finely chopped green onions

Assorted crackers

In a small bowl, combine the cheeses, parsley, mayonnaise, salt, cayenne, pepper and food coloring if desired; beat until smooth. Stir in cucumber and onion. Chill until serving. Serve with crackers.

crunchy caramel corn

PREP: 10 min. + cooling | **YIELD:** about 2 quarts.

My sweet and crunchy popcorn gets gobbled up fast at parties and get-togethers.
SHELY GROMER, LONG BEACH, CALIFORNIA

6	cups popped popcorn
3/4	cup salted peanuts
1/2	cup packed brown sugar
1/4	cup butter, cubed
2	tablespoons light corn syrup
1/4	teaspoon salt
1/2	teaspoon vanilla extract
1/4	teaspoon baking soda

Place popcorn and peanuts in a large microwave-safe bowl; set aside. In another microwave-safe bowl, combine the brown sugar, butter, corn syrup and salt. Cover and microwave on high for 30-60 seconds; stir. Microwave 1-1/2 minutes longer.

Stir in vanilla and baking soda. Pour over popcorn mixture. Microwave, uncovered, on high for 2 minutes, stirring several times. Spread on greased baking sheets to cool. Store in an airtight container.

EDITOR'S NOTE: This recipe was tested in a 1,100-watt microwave.

mint juleps

PREP: 30 min. + chilling | **YIELD:** 10 servings (2-1/2 cups syrup).

This classic Kentucky Derby beverage features the perfect blend of mint, bourbon and sugar. Down south, this refreshing cooler is nearly as famous as sweet tea. Mint juleps are traditionally served in a silver or pewter mug, but you can also enjoy them in a rocks glass with a straw.
TASTE OF HOME TEST KITCHEN

MINT SYRUP:

2	cups sugar
2	cups water
2	cups loosely packed chopped fresh mint

EACH SERVING:

1/2	to 3/4 cup crushed ice
1/2	to 1 ounce bourbon

Mint sprig

For syrup, combine the sugar, water and chopped mint in a large saucepan. Bring to a boil over medium heat; cook until sugar is dissolved, stirring occasionally. Remove from the heat; cool to room temperature.

Line a mesh strainer with a double layer of cheesecloth or a coffee filter. Strain syrup; discard mint. Cover and refrigerate syrup for at least 2 hours or until chilled.

For each serving, place ice in a metal julep cup or rocks glass. Pour 1/4 cup mint syrup and bourbon into the glass; stir until mixture is well chilled. Garnish with mint sprig.

MOCK MINT JULEP: Prepare mint syrup as directed. After straining, add 1/2 cup lemon juice. Cover and refrigerate for at least 2 hours or until chilled. For each serving, combine 1/2 cup club soda and 1/4 cup mint syrup in a glass filled with crushed ice. Garnish with mint.

mint juleps

grits 'n' shrimp tarts

PREP/TOTAL TIME: 30 min. | **YIELD:** 2-1/2 dozen.

This deliciously different appetizer showcases two Mississippi staples—grits and shrimp. I guarantee your family will enjoy them as much as mine!

ELIZABETH LATADY, JACKSON, MISSISSIPPI

1	cup water
1/4	cup quick-cooking grits
2	ounces cream cheese, softened
1/4	cup shredded cheddar cheese
3	tablespoons butter, *divided*
1/4	teaspoon garlic salt
1/8	teaspoon salt

Pepper to taste

1	pound uncooked small shrimp, peeled and deveined
3	green onions, sliced
2	packages (1.9 ounces *each*) frozen miniature phyllo tart shells

In a small saucepan, bring water to a boil. Gradually stir in grits. Reduce heat; cover and simmer for 4 minutes. Stir in the cheeses, 1 tablespoon butter, garlic salt, salt and pepper.

In a large skillet, saute shrimp and onions in remaining butter until shrimp turn pink. Fill tart shells with grits; top with shrimp mixture. Refrigerate leftovers.

peeling and deveining shrimp

Start on the underside by the head area to remove shell from shrimp. Pull legs and first section of shell to one side. Continue pulling shell up around the top and to the other side. Pull off shell by tail if desired. Remove the black vein running down the back of shrimp by making a shallow slit with a paring knife along the back from head area to tail. Rinse shrimp under cold water to remove the vein.

oysters rockefeller

PREP: 1-1/4 hours | **BAKE:** 10 min. | **YIELD:** 3 dozen.

In 1899, Jules Alciatore created the French-inspired Oysters Rockefeller to serve in his father's New Orleans restaurant. The famous baked oyster dish is named after John D. Rockefeller, the wealthiest man of the time, because of the richness of the sauce.
BETH WALTON, EASTHAM, MASSACHUSETTS

3	dozen fresh oysters in the shell, washed
1	medium onion, finely chopped
1/2	cup butter, cubed
1	package (9 ounces) fresh spinach, torn
1	cup grated Romano cheese
1	tablespoon lemon juice
1/8	teaspoon pepper
2	pounds kosher salt

Shuck oysters, reserving bottom shell; set aside. In a large skillet, saute onion in butter until tender. Add spinach; cook and stir until wilted. Remove from the heat; stir in the cheese, lemon juice and pepper.

Spread kosher salt into two ungreased 15-in. x 10-in. x 1-in. baking pans. Lightly press the oyster shells down into the salt. Place one oyster in each shell; top each with 2-1/2 teaspoons spinach mixture.

Bake, uncovered, at 450° for 6-8 minutes or until oysters are plump. Serve immediately.

texas caviar

PREP: 20 min. + chilling | **YIELD:** 5 cups.

I adapted this recipe from one I found in a cookbook. We can't get enough of this Southwestern sensation.
BECKY OLIVER, FAIRPLAY, COLORADO

2	cans (15-1/2 ounces each) black-eyed peas, rinsed and drained
1	can (10 ounces) diced tomatoes and green chilies, drained
1	medium green pepper, finely chopped
1	small red onion, finely chopped
1/2	cup fat-free Italian salad dressing
2	tablespoons lime juice
1/4	teaspoon salt
1/4	teaspoon pepper
1	medium ripe avocado, peeled and cubed

Tortilla chips

In a large bowl, combine the peas, tomatoes, green pepper and onion. In a small bowl, whisk the dressing, lime juice, salt and pepper. Pour over black-eyed pea mixture and stir to coat. Cover and refrigerate for at least 1 hour.

Stir in avocado just before serving. Serve with chips.

fresh lime margaritas

PREP/TOTAL TIME: 15 min. | **YIELD:** 4 servings.

This basic margarita recipe is easy to modify to suit your tastes. Try it with strawberries or raspberries.
TASTE OF HOME TEST KITCHEN

4	lime wedges
1	tablespoon kosher salt
1/2	cup gold tequila
1/4	cup Triple Sec
1/4	cup lime juice
1/4	cup lemon juice
2	tablespoons superfine sugar
1-1/3	cups crushed ice

Using lime wedges, moisten rims of four glasses. Holding each glass upside down, dip rim into salt; set aside.

In a pitcher, combine the tequila, Triple Sec, lime juice, lemon juice and sugar; stir until sugar is dissolved. Serve in prepared glasses over crushed ice.

FOR FROZEN LIME MARGARITAS: Reduce lemon and lime juices to 2 tablespoons each. Increase the superfine sugar to 1/4 cup and the crushed ice to 4 cups. Add 3/4 cup limeade concentrate. Prepare glasses as directed. In a blender, combine the tequila, Triple Sec, lime juice, lemon juice, limeade concentrate, superfine sugar and crushed ice; cover and process until smooth. Yield: 5 cups.

FOR FROZEN BERRY MARGARITAS: Follow directions for Frozen Lime Margaritas, except reduce crushed ice to 2 cups and add 2 cups frozen unsweetened berries. Yield: 4 cups.

fresh lime margaritas

pimiento cheese spread

PREP: 10 min. + chilling | **YIELD:** 1-1/4 cups.

A classic Southern comfort food, this spread is used as a dip for crackers, corn chips or celery. It is also commonly smeared between two slices of white bread for sandwiches and used as a topping for hamburgers and hot dogs.

EILEEN BALMER, SOUTH BEND, INDIANA

- 1-1/2 cups (6 ounces) shredded cheddar cheese
- 1 jar (4 ounces) diced pimientos, drained and finely chopped
- 1/3 cup mayonnaise
- Assorted crackers

In a small bowl, combine the cheese, pimientos and mayonnaise. Refrigerate for at least 1 hour. Serve with assorted crackers.

spiced peanuts

PREP: 10 min. | **BAKE:** 20 min. | **YIELD:** 3 cups.

Liven up plain peanuts with a sweet-and-spicy blend of sugar, cumin and cayenne pepper. They go fast so you may want to double or triple the recipe!

HOLLY KUNKLE, WALTON, KENTUCKY

- 1 jar (16 ounces) unsalted dry roasted peanuts
- 2 tablespoons canola oil
- 2 tablespoons sugar
- 1-1/2 teaspoons ground cumin
- 1 teaspoon salt
- 1/2 teaspoon cayenne pepper
- 1/2 teaspoon garlic powder

Place peanuts in a small bowl; drizzle with oil and toss to coat. Combine sugar and seasonings; sprinkle over nuts and

spiced peanuts

avocado shrimp salsa

toss to coat. Transfer to an ungreased 15-in. x 10-in. x 1-in. baking pan. Bake at 300° for 20-25 minutes or until lightly browned, stirring occasionally. Spread on waxed paper to cool. Store in an airtight container.

avocado shrimp salsa

PREP/TOTAL TIME: 25 min. 6 cups.

This is salsa, Southern-style! It's delicious scooped up with tortilla chips or atop grilled chicken breasts or pork chops. You can even eat it as a chunky side dish alongside your favorite entree.

MARIA SIMMONS, RIO RANCHO, NEW MEXICO

- 1 pound cooked small shrimp, peeled, deveined and chopped
- 2 medium tomatoes, seeded and chopped
- 2 medium ripe avocados, peeled and chopped
- 1 cup minced fresh cilantro
- 1 medium sweet red pepper, chopped
- 3/4 cup thinly sliced green onions
- 1/2 cup chopped seeded peeled cucumber
- 3 tablespoons lime juice
- 1 jalapeno pepper, seeded and chopped
- 1 teaspoon salt
- 1/4 teaspoon pepper
- Tortilla chips

In a large bowl, combine the first 11 ingredients. Serve with tortilla chips.

EDITOR'S NOTE: We recommend wearing disposable gloves when cutting hot peppers. Avoid touching your face.

crispy chicken fingers

PREP: 20 min. | **COOK:** 5 min./batch | **YIELD:** 7 servings.

My hungry clan devours these moist, tender chicken strips. You can enjoy them dipped them in honey mustard or ranch dressing or cut up into pieces and tossed over a salad.

RACHEL FIZEL, WOODBURY, MINNESOTA

1	cup all-purpose flour
1	cup dry bread crumbs
2	tablespoons grated Parmesan cheese
1	teaspoon salt
3/4	teaspoon garlic powder
1/2	teaspoon baking powder
1	egg
1	cup buttermilk
1-3/4	pounds boneless skinless chicken breasts, cut into strips

Oil for deep-fat frying

In a large resealable plastic bag, combine the first six ingredients. In a shallow bowl, whisk egg and buttermilk. Dip a few pieces of chicken at a time in buttermilk mixture, then place in bag; seal and shake to coat.

In an electric skillet, heat oil to 375°. Fry chicken, a few strips at a time, for 2-3 minutes on each side or until a meat thermometer reads 170°. Drain on paper towels.

bread crumbs

You can easily make your own soft bread crumbs from fresh or slightly stale bread. Simply tear the bread apart with a fork or use a blender or food processor to break it up into fluffy crumbs. Spoon gently into a measuring cup, but do not pack.

Dry bread crumbs may be purchased or made from very dry bread or zwieback crackers. Place in a plastic bag and crush with a rolling pin. Spoon into a measuring cup.

18   19   22   25

BANANA NUT BREAD

breads & biscuits

banana nut bread

PREP: 10 min. | **BAKE:** 40 min. + cooling
YIELD: 2 loaves (12 slices each).

After years of searching, I finally found the perfect banana bread! A basic yellow cake mix streamlines assembly so I can have it ready in a jiffy. The recipe yields two loaves, so we can eat one right away and save the other in the freezer to enjoy later.
MARIE DAVIS, PENDLETON, SOUTH CAROLINA

1	package (18-1/4 ounces) yellow cake mix
1	egg
1/2	cup 2% milk
1	cup mashed ripe bananas (about 2 medium)
1/2	cup chopped pecans

In a large bowl, combine the cake mix, egg and milk. Add the bananas; beat mixture on medium speed for 2 minutes. Stir in the pecans.

Pour into two greased 8-in. x 4-in. loaf pans. Bake at 350° for 40-45 minutes or until a toothpick inserted near the center comes out clean. Cool for 10 minutes before removing from pans to wire racks to cool completely.

down home hush puppies

PREP: 15 min. + standing | **COOK:** 20 min. | **YIELD:** 2-1/2 dozen.

Hush puppies are deep-friend corn bread balls typically served alongside seafood. Their sweet and spicy flavor has delighted folks for decades.
GENE PITTS, WILSONVILLE, ALABAMA

1	cup cornmeal
1	cup self-rising flour
1-1/2	teaspoons baking powder
1/2	teaspoon salt
1	large onion, chopped
2	jalapeno peppers, seeded and diced
1/4	cup sugar
1	egg
1	cup buttermilk

Canola oil

In a large bowl, combine the first seven ingredients. Add the egg and buttermilk; stir until the dry ingredients are moistened. Set aside at room temperature for 30 minutes. Do not stir again.

In an electric skillet or deep fryer, heat 2-3 in. of oil to 375°. Drop batter by rounded tablespoonfuls, a few at a time, into hot oil. Fry until golden brown, about 1-1/2 minutes on each side. Drain on paper towels.

EDITOR'S NOTE: As a substitute for 1 cup of self-rising flour, place 1-1/2 teaspoons baking powder and 1/2 teaspoon salt in a measuring cup. Add all-purpose flour to measure 1 cup.

ham 'n' corn fritters

ham 'n' corn fritters

PREP: 20 min. + standing | **COOK:** 15 min. | **YIELD:** 2 dozen.

Here's an old-fashioned recipe that's welcome at any meal. The pretty golden fritters are a perfect addition to a homey brunch. You'll be amazed at how quickly they disappear from the table.
NELDA CRONBAUGH, BELLE PLAINE, IOWA

2	eggs
1/3	cup milk
1-1/4	cups all-purpose flour
1	tablespoon sugar
2	teaspoons baking powder
1/2	teaspoon salt

Dash pepper

1	cup fresh *or* frozen corn, cooked and drained
1	cup chopped fully cooked ham

Oil for deep-fat frying

Separate eggs; let stand at room temperature for 30 minutes. In a large bowl, beat egg yolks until slightly thickened. Beat in milk. Combine the flour, sugar, baking powder, salt and pepper; add to the yolk mixture and mix well. Stir in the corn and ham.

In a small bowl, beat egg whites on high speed until stiff peaks form. Fold into the corn mixture.

In an electric skillet or deep-fat fryer, heat oil to 375°. Drop batter by heaping tablespoonfuls, a few at a time, into hot oil. Fry until golden brown, about 1 minute on each side, turning with a slotted spoon. Drain on paper towels.

cappuccino cinnamon rolls

PREP: 45 min. + rising | **BAKE:** 25 min. | **YIELD:** 1 dozen.

A distinctive coffee flavor accents the filling of these ooey, gooey rolls. Spread on the sweet glaze while they're still warm...they won't last long!

SHERRI COX, LUCASVILLE, OHIO

1	package (1/4 ounce) active dry yeast
1	cup warm water (110° to 115°)
3/4	cup warm milk (110° to 115°)
1/2	cup buttermilk
3	tablespoons sugar
2	tablespoons butter, softened
1-1/4	teaspoons salt
5-1/2	to 6 cups all-purpose flour

FILLING:

1/4	cup butter, melted
1	cup packed brown sugar
4	teaspoons instant coffee granules
2	teaspoons ground cinnamon

ICING:

2	tablespoons butter, softened
1	to 2 tablespoons milk
2	teaspoons cappuccino mix
1-1/2	cups confectioners' sugar
1/2	teaspoon vanilla extract

In a large bowl, dissolve yeast in warm water. Add the warm milk, buttermilk, sugar, butter, salt and 4 cups flour. Beat on medium speed until smooth. Stir in enough remaining flour to form a soft dough (dough will be sticky).

Turn onto a floured surface; knead until smooth and elastic, about 6-8 minutes. Place in a greased bowl, turning once to grease the top. Cover and let rise in a warm place until doubled, about 1 hour.

Punch dough down; turn onto a floured surface. Roll into an 18-in. x 12-in. rectangle; brush with butter. Combine the brown sugar, coffee granules and cinnamon; sprinkle over dough to within 1/2 in. of edges.

Roll up jelly-roll style, starting with a long side; pinch seam to seal. Cut into 12 slices. Place rolls, cut side down, in a greased 13-in. x 9-in. baking pan. Cover and let rise until doubled, about 30 minutes.

Bake at 350° for 22-28 minutes or until golden brown. Place pan on a wire rack. In a small bowl, beat the icing ingredients until smooth. Spread over warm rolls. Serve warm.

raspberry crumble coffee cake

PREP: 20 min. | **BAKE:** 45 min. | **YIELD:** 16-20 servings.

Don't let these recipe instructions intimidate you—this coffee cake is easier than it looks. It makes a lovely addition to brunch or a delicious dessert.

SHIRLEY BOYKEN, MESA, ARIZONA

FILLING:

2/3	cup sugar
1/4	cup cornstarch
3/4	cup water *or* cranberry-raspberry juice
2	cups fresh *or* frozen unsweetened raspberries
1	tablespoon lemon juice

COFFEE CAKE:

3	cups all-purpose flour
1	cup sugar
3	teaspoons baking powder
1	teaspoon salt
1	teaspoon ground cinnamon
1/4	teaspoon ground mace
1	cup cold butter, cubed
2	eggs, lightly beaten
1	cup milk
1	teaspoon vanilla extract

TOPPING:

1/4	cup cold butter, cubed
1/2	cup all-purpose flour
1/2	cup sugar
1/4	cup sliced almonds

For filling, in a large saucepan, combine the sugar, cornstarch and water until smooth. Bring to a boil over medium heat. Cook and stir for 1-2 minutes or until thickened. Add berries and lemon juice. Set aside to cool.

In a large bowl, combine the flour, sugar, baking powder, salt, cinnamon and mace. Cut in butter to form fine crumbs. Stir in the eggs, milk and vanilla until blended. Divide in half.

Spread half of the batter in two greased 8-in. round baking pans. Divide filling and spread evenly over each. Drop remaining batter by small spoonfuls and spread evenly over filling.

For topping, cut butter into flour and sugar; stir in nuts. Sprinkle over tops. Bake at 350° for 40-45 minutes or until lightly brown.

EDITOR'S NOTE: If desired, one coffee cake can be baked in 13-in. x 9-in. baking pan. Bake for 45-50 minutes or until golden brown.

buttermilk corn bread

PREP/TOTAL TIME: 30 min. | **YIELD:** 2-4 servings.

My grandmother made this corn bread using farm-fresh eggs and staples found in the pantry. She always cooked it in her famous black skillet, and it turned out slick as butter every time.

ELIZABETH COOPER, MADISON, ALABAMA

1	tablespoon canola oil
1	cup cornmeal
1/4	cup all-purpose flour
1-1/2	teaspoons baking powder
1/2	teaspoon salt
1/2	teaspoon baking soda
1	egg
1	cup buttermilk

Place oil in an 8-in. ovenproof skillet; tilt to coat bottom and sides. Place in a 425° oven for 10 minutes.

In a small bowl, combine cornmeal, flour, baking powder, salt and baking soda. Beat egg and buttermilk; add to dry ingredients just until moistened.

Pour batter into the hot skillet. Bake for 15 minutes or until golden brown and a toothpick inserted near the center comes out clean.

buttermilk corn bread

storing baked goods

Cool coffee cakes, sweet rolls and other bakery treats completely before storing. Place in an airtight container or plastic bag; keep at room temperature for 2 to 3 days. Breads containing perishable items should be refrigerated. For longer storage, unfrosted sweet breads can be frozen for up to 3 months. When ready to eat, thaw at room temperature, then frost or glaze as desired.

spiced fruited hot cross buns

PREP: 40 min. + rising | **BAKE:** 20 min. | **YIELD:** 2 dozen.

It's tradition to serve hot cross buns in the spring, but with my easy recipe you'll want to serve them all year long! The bread machine does all the hard work, so you'll be left with a decadent treat that tastes like you fussed.
ALINA NIEMI, HONOLULU, HAWAII

1-1/2	cups fat-free milk (70° to 80°)
1/4	cup water (70° to 80°)
1/4	cup butter, melted
1	teaspoon salt
2/3	cup sugar
2	tablespoons ground flaxseed
1	tablespoon grated orange peel
2	teaspoons grated lemon peel
1/4	teaspoon *each* ground cardamom, cinnamon and nutmeg
2-1/4	cups whole wheat flour
2	cups all-purpose flour
1	package (1/4 ounce) active dry yeast
1/2	cup golden raisins
1/4	cup dried cranberries
1/4	cup chopped crystallized ginger

ICING:

3/4	cup confectioners' sugar
3/4	teaspoon grated orange peel
2	to 3 teaspoons lemon juice

In bread machine pan, place the first 14 ingredients in order suggested by manufacturer. Select dough setting (check dough after 5 minutes of mixing; add 1 to 2 tablespoons of water or flour if needed). Before the final kneading (your

cheesy drop biscuits

machine may audibly signal this), add the raisins, cranberries and candied ginger.

When cycle is completed, turn dough onto a lightly floured surface. Divide into 24 portions; shape each into a ball. Place 2 in. apart on baking sheets coated with cooking spray. Cover and let rise in a warm place until doubled, about 40 minutes.

Bake at 350° for 20-25 minutes or until golden brown. Remove from pans to wire racks. Combine the icing ingredients; pipe an "X" on each bun.

cheesy drop biscuits

PREP/TOTAL TIME: 30 min. | **YIELD:** 2 dozen.

I always keep the ingredients for these buttery bites on hand so I can make them whenever we get a hankering for something warm and cheesy.
MARLA MILLER, ENGLEWOOD, TENNESSEE

2	cups self-rising flour
1	cup butter, melted
1	cup (8 ounces) sour cream
1	cup (4 ounces) shredded cheddar cheese

In a large bowl, combine all the ingredients until blended. Drop by rounded tablespoonfuls 2 in. apart onto lightly greased baking sheets.

Bake at 350° for 20-25 minutes or until golden brown. Cool for 5 minutes before removing from pans to wire racks. Serve warm.

EDITOR'S NOTE: As a substitute for each cup of self-rising flour, place 1-1/2 teaspoons baking powder and 1/2 teaspoon salt in a measuring cup. Add all-purpose flour to measure 1 cup.

spiced fruited hot cross buns

grandma's orange rolls

PREP: 20 min. + rising | **BAKE:** 20 min. | **YIELD:** 2-1/2 dozen.

My family loves these fine-textured rolls featuring a burst of citrus. We live in Florida, and we're lucky to have the pleasure of picking fresh fruit right off our own orange, lime and grapefruit trees.

NORMA POOLE, AUBURNDALE, FLORIDA

- 1 package (1/4 ounce) active dry yeast
- 1/4 cup warm water (110° to 115°)
- 1 cup warm milk (110° to 115°)
- 1/4 cup shortening
- 1/4 cup sugar
- 1 teaspoon salt
- 1 egg, lightly beaten
- 3-1/2 to 3-3/4 cups all-purpose flour

FILLING:
- 1 cup sugar
- 1/2 cup butter, softened
- 2 tablespoons grated orange peel

GLAZE:
- 1 cup confectioners' sugar
- 4 teaspoons butter, softened
- 4 to 5 teaspoons milk
- 1/2 teaspoon lemon extract

In a large bowl, dissolve the yeast in water. Add the milk, shortening, sugar, salt, egg and 3 cups flour. Beat until smooth. Stir in enough remaining flour to form a soft dough.

Knead on a lightly floured surface until smooth and elastic, about 6-8 minutes. Place in a greased bowl, turning once to grease top. Cover and let rise in a warm place until doubled, about 1 hour. Meanwhile, in a small bowl, combine filling ingredients; set aside.

Punch dough down; divide in half. Roll each half into a 15-in. x 10-in. rectangle. Spread half the reserved filling on each

grandma's orange rolls

buttermilk pan rolls

rectangle. Roll up, jelly-roll style, starting with a long end. Cut each into 15 rolls.

Place in two greased 11-in. x 7-in. baking pans. Cover and let rise until doubled, about 45 minutes.

Bake at 375° for 20-25 minutes or until lightly browned. In a small bowl, combine glaze ingredients until smooth; spread over warm rolls.

buttermilk pan rolls

PREP: 20 min. + rising | **BAKE:** 20 min. | **YIELD:** 2 dozen.

These classic rolls can be made in a jiffy and go well with any main dish.

PATRICIA YOUNG, BELLA VISTA, ARKANSAS

- 2 packages (1/4 ounce *each*) active dry yeast
- 1/4 cup warm water (110° to 115°)
- 1-1/2 cups warm buttermilk (110° to 115°)
- 1/2 cup canola oil
- 3 tablespoons sugar
- 4-1/2 cups all-purpose flour
- 1 teaspoon baking soda
- 1/2 teaspoon salt

In a large bowl, dissolve yeast in warm water. Add the buttermilk, oil and sugar. Combine the flour, baking soda and salt; add to yeast mixture and beat until smooth. Do not knead. Let stand for 10 minutes.

Turn dough onto a lightly floured surface; punch down. Shape into 24 balls and place in two greased 9-in. square baking pans. Cover and let rise in a warm place until doubled, about 30 minutes.

Bake at 400° for 20 minutes or until golden brown. Remove from pans to wire racks to cool.

EDITOR'S NOTE: Warmed buttermilk will appear curdled.

english batter buns

PREP: 15 min. + rising | **BAKE:** 10 min. | **YIELD:** 1 dozen.

These rich, slighlty sweet yeast buns are similar to traditional Sally Lunn bread. I serve them every year around the holidays. GERALDINE WEST, OGDEN, UTAH

2	packages (1/4 ounces *each*) active dry yeast
1	cup warm milk (110° to 115°)
1/2	cup shortening
2	tablespoons sugar
1	teaspoon salt
2	eggs, lightly beaten
3-1/2	cups all-purpose flour
Melted butter	

In a bowl, dissolve yeast in warm milk. Add the shortening, sugar, salt, eggs and 2 cups flour; beat on medium speed for 3 minutes. Stir in remaining flour until smooth. Cover and let rise in a warm place until doubled, about 30 minutes.

Stir batter vigorously for 25 strokes (dough will be slightly sticky). Spoon into greased muffin cups. Tap pans to settle the batter. Cover and let rise until batter reaches tops of cups, about 20 minutes.

Bake at 400° for 10-15 minutes. Brush with butter.

sally lunn bread

Sally Lunn bread was brought to the United States from England and subsequently became popular in the South. Local folklore suggests that Sally Lunn, an 18th-century baker from Bath, England, created this French-inspired bread for her prominent patrons' tea parties. Although it's classically baked in a tube pan, it can also be made in loaves and buns. In fact, the original cake-like treat was baked as large buns, split in half and spread with thick cream.

overnight refrigerator rolls

PREP: 25 min. + chilling | **BAKE:** 15 min. | **YIELD:** 1 dozen.

My simple-to-fix dinner rolls couldn't be tastier. Their buttery flavor makes them a heartwarming accompaniment to soups, salads and a variety of main dishes.

JENNIFER KAUFFMAN FIGUEROA
GREENVILLE, SOUTH CAROLINA

1	package (1/4 ounce) active dry yeast
1/2	cup warm water (110° to 115°)
1/2	cup warm 2% milk (110° to 115°)
1/4	cup butter-flavored shortening
1	tablespoon sugar
1	teaspoon salt
1	egg
3	cups all-purpose flour

In a large bowl, dissolve yeast in warm water. Add the milk, shortening, sugar, salt, egg and 2 cups flour. Beat on medium speed for 2 minutes. Stir in enough remaining flour to form a soft dough (do not knead). Place in a greased bowl, turning once to grease the top. Cover and refrigerate overnight.

Punch dough down. Turn onto a lightly floured surface; divide into 12 pieces. Shape each into a ball. Place 2 in. apart on greased baking sheets. Cover and let rise in a warm place until doubled, about 1-1/2 hours.

Bake at 400° for 15-20 minutes or until golden brown. Remove from pans to wire racks.

overnight refrigerator rolls

pecan sticky buns

PREP: 45 min. + rising | **BAKE:** 20 min. | **YIELD:** 1 dozen.

These tender, nutty caramel rolls feature the old-fashioned Southern goodness my family craves. Try one of the three variations for a change of pace.
JULIA SPENCE, NEW BRAUNFELS, TEXAS

- 4 to 4-1/2 cups all-purpose flour
- 1/3 cup sugar
- 1 package (1/4 ounce) active dry yeast
- 1/2 teaspoon salt
- 1 cup 2% milk
- 1/4 cup butter, cubed
- 2 eggs

TOPPING:
- 1/3 cup butter, cubed
- 2/3 cup packed brown sugar
- 2 tablespoons light corn syrup
- 1 cup chopped pecans

FILLING:
- 3 tablespoons butter, melted
- 1/2 cup packed brown sugar
- 1/3 cup sugar
- 2 tablespoons ground cinnamon

In a large bowl, combine 2 cups flour, sugar, yeast and salt. In a small saucepan, heat milk and butter to 120°-130°. Add to dry ingredients; beat just until moistened. Add eggs; beat until smooth. Stir in enough remaining flour to form a soft dough (dough will be sticky).

Turn onto a floured surface; knead until smooth and elastic, about 6-8 minutes. Place in a greased bowl, turning once to grease top. Cover and let rise in a warm place until doubled, about 1 hour.

In a small saucepan, melt butter over medium heat. Stir in brown sugar and corn syrup until combined. Pour into a well-greased 13-in. x 9-in. baking dish. Sprinkle with pecans.

Punch dough down. Turn onto a floured surface. Roll into a 12-in. x 8-in. rectangle; brush with melted butter. Combine sugars and cinnamon; sprinkle over dough to within 1/2 in. of edges and press into dough. Roll up jelly-roll style, starting with a long side; pinch seam to seal.

Cut into 12 slices. Place cut side down in prepared pan. Cover and let rise until doubled, about 30 minutes.

Bake at 375° for 20-25 minutes or until golden brown. Immediately invert onto a serving platter. Serve warm.

CINNAMON ROLLS: Omit topping. Frost warm rolls with Vanilla Frosting: Combine 1-1/2 cups confectioners' sugar, 3 tablespoons softened butter, 3/4 teaspoon vanilla extract and about 1 tablespoon milk.

CHOCOLATE CHIP CINNAMON ROLLS: Omit topping and filling. Brush dough with 2 tablespoons melted butter. Combine 1/4 cup packed brown sugar, 1/2 teaspoon ground cinnamon and 2/3 cup miniature semisweet chocolate chips; sprinkle over dough. Frost warm rolls with vanilla frosting (see Cinnamon Rolls variation above).

HOT BUTTER RUM ROLLS: Add 1/2 teaspoon rum extract to topping. Omit cinnamon from filling. Add 1/3 cup chopped pecans and 1/2 teaspoon rum extract to filling.

apple pull-apart bread

PREP: 40 min. + rising | **BAKE:** 35 min. + cooling
YIELD: 1 loaf.

Drizzled with icing, each finger-licking piece of this bread has a delicious filling of apples and pecans. Friends and family will love it.

CAROLYN GREGORY, HENDERSONVILLE, TENNESSEE

- 1 package (1/4 ounce) active dry yeast
- 1 cup warm milk
- 1/2 cup butter, melted, *divided*
- 1 egg
- 2/3 cup plus 2 tablespoons sugar, *divided*
- 1 teaspoon salt
- 3 to 3-1/2 cups all-purpose flour
- 1 medium tart apple, peeled and chopped
- 1/2 cup finely chopped pecans
- 1/2 teaspoon ground cinnamon

ICING:

- 1 cup confectioners' sugar
- 3 to 4-1/2 teaspoons hot water
- 1/2 teaspoon vanilla extract

In a large bowl, dissolve yeast in milk. Add 2 tablespoons butter, egg, 2 tablespoons sugar, salt and 3 cups flour; beat until smooth. Add enough remaining flour to form a stiff dough. Turn onto a floured surface; knead until smooth and elastic, 6-8 minutes. Place in a greased bowl, turning once to grease top. Cover and let rise in a warm place until doubled, about 1 hour.

Combine the apple, pecans, cinnamon and remaining sugar; set aside. Punch dough down; divide in half. Cut each half into 16 pieces. On a lightly floured surface, pat or roll out each piece into a 2-1/2-in. circle. Place 1 teaspoon apple mixture in center of circle; pinch edges together and seal, forming a ball. Dip in remaining butter.

In a greased 10-in. tube pan, place 16 balls, seam side down; sprinkle with 1/4 cup apple mixture. Layer remaining balls; sprinkle with remaining apple mixture. Cover and let rise until nearly doubled, about 45 minutes.

Bake at 350° for 35-40 minutes or until golden brown. Cool for 10 minutes; remove from pan to a wire rack. Combine icing ingredients; drizzle over warm bread.

apple pull-apart bread

good ol' banana muffins

PREP/TOTAL TIME: 30 min. | **YIELD:** 14 muffins.

Love banana bread? Then you're sure to like these golden muffins. They're a great treat anytime you crave that scrumptious old-fashioned flavor.

CLYDE BLOUNT, PEARL, MISSISSIPPI

- 1/2 cup butter, softened
- 1 cup sugar
- 2 eggs
- 3 medium ripe bananas, mashed
- 2 cups self-rising flour
- 1 teaspoon baking soda
- 1/2 cup chopped pecans

In a large bowl, cream butter and sugar until light and fluffy. Add eggs, one at a time, beating well after each addition. Beat in bananas. Combine flour and baking soda; add to creamed mixture just until moistened. Fold in pecans.

Fill greased or paper-lined muffin cups three-fourths full. Bake at 350° for 20-25 minutes or until a toothpick inserted near the center comes out clean. Cool for 5 minutes before removing from pans to wire racks.

EDITOR'S NOTE: As a substitute for each cup of self-rising flour, place 1-1/2 teaspoons baking powder and 1/2 teaspoon salt in a measuring cup. Add all-purpose flour to measure 1 cup.

freezing bananas

Have bananas but no time to bake? Peel and mash overripe bananas with 1 teaspoon of lemon juice for each banana used. Freeze in 1- or 2-cup amounts in airtight containers for up to 6 months. Pull out of the freezer when you have time to bake banana bread or muffins. About 1-1/3 cups mashed banana equals three medium or four small bananas.

quick blueberry muffins

PREP: 15 min. | **BAKE:** 25 min. | **YIELD:** 6 servings.

The addition of ice cream yields a yummy vanilla flavor to these cake-like baked treats.

AMY LOU STRICKLAND, MARTINEZ, GEORGIA

1	**cup vanilla ice cream, softened**
1	**cup self-rising flour**
1	**cup fresh blueberries**
1	**tablespoon butter**
2	**tablespoons sugar**

In a large bowl, combine ice cream and flour. Fold in blueberries. Spoon into six greased muffin cups.

Bake at 375° for 20-25 minutes or until a toothpick inserted near the center comes out clean. While hot, brush muffin tops with butter and sprinkle with sugar. Serve warm.

spoon muffins

PREP: 15 min. | **BAKE:** 20 min. | **YIELD:** 2-1/2 to 3 dozen.

This muffin recipe is one of my all-time favorites. I like to make them plain or studded with blueberries. No matter how they're prepared, these little gems are best hot from the oven and slathered with sweet, creamy butter!

TREVA LATTA, VALLEY CENTER, KANSAS

1	**package (1/4 ounce) active dry yeast**
2	**cups warm water (110° to 115°)**
4	**cups self-rising flour**
1	**egg, lightly beaten**
3/4	**cup butter**
1/4	**cup sugar**

In a large bowl, dissolve yeast in warm water; let stand for 5 minutes. Combine the flour, egg, butter and sugar; add to yeast mixture and mix well.

Fill greased or paper-lined muffin cups two-thirds full. Bake at 400° for 20-25 minutes or until a toothpick inserted near the center comes out clean.

southern buttermilk biscuits

PREP/TOTAL TIME: 30 min. | **YIELD:** 9 biscuits.

This classic biscuit makes a great accompaniment to fried chicken or any favorite main entree.

FRAN THOMPSON, TARBORO, NORTH CAROLINA

1/2	**cup cold butter, cubed**
2	**cups self-rising flour**
3/4	**cup buttermilk**

Melted butter

In a large bowl, cut butter into flour until mixture resembles coarse crumbs. Stir in buttermilk just until moistened. Turn onto a lightly floured surface; knead 3-4 times. Pat or lightly roll to 3/4-in. thickness. Cut dough with a floured 2-1/2-in. biscuit cutter.

Place biscuits on a greased baking sheet. Bake at 425° for 11-13 minutes or until golden brown. Brush tops with butter. Serve warm.

EDITOR'S NOTE: As a substitute for each cup of self-rising flour, place 1-1/2 teaspoons baking powder and 1/2 teaspoon salt in a measuring cup. Add all-purpose flour to measure 1 cup.

ZESTY TORTILLA SOUP

soups, stews &chili

zesty tortilla soup

PREP: 20 min. | **COOK:** 1-3/4 hours
YIELD: 10 servings (2-1/2 quarts).

My family has a penchant for Southwestern fare, so this soup often makes an appearance on our table. It has just the right amount of spice.
TAMMY LEIBER, NAVASOTA, TEXAS

- 1 medium onion, chopped
- 2 tablespoons canola oil
- 2 garlic cloves, minced
- 2 pounds beef stew meat, cut into 1-inch cubes
- 2 cups water
- 1 can (14-1/2 ounces) stewed tomatoes
- 1 can (10 ounces) diced tomatoes with green chilies, undrained
- 1 can (10-3/4 ounces) condensed tomato soup, undiluted
- 1 can (10-1/2 ounces) beef broth
- 1 can (10-1/2 ounces) chicken broth
- 1 tablespoon Worcestershire sauce
- 1 teaspoon ground cumin
- 1 teaspoon chili powder
- 1 teaspoon salt
- 1 teaspoon lemon-pepper seasoning
- 1/2 teaspoon hot pepper sauce
- 10 corn tortillas (6 inches)

Shredded cheddar cheese, sour cream and sliced green onions, optional

In a Dutch oven, saute onion in oil until tender. Add garlic; cook 1 minute longer. Stir in the next 13 ingredients; bring to a boil. Reduce heat; cover and simmer for 1-1/2 hours or until beef is tender.

Tear the tortillas into bite-size pieces; add to soup. Simmer, uncovered, for 10 minutes; let stand for 5 minutes. Garnish individual servings with the cheese, sour cream and onions if desired.

ham and bean soup

PREP: 30 min. + soaking | **COOK:** 1-1/2 hours
YIELD: 15 servings (3-3/4 quarts).

I learned to make this soup when we lived in Pennsylvania near several Amish families. It's a great way to use up ham and mashed potatoes. Best of all, it freezes well.
AMANDA REED, MILFORD, DELAWARE

- 1 pound dried navy beans
- 2 medium onions, chopped
- 2 teaspoons canola oil
- 2 celery ribs, chopped
- 10 cups water
- 4 cups cubed fully cooked ham
- 1 cup mashed potatoes (without added milk and butter)
- 1/2 cup shredded carrot
- 2 tablespoons Worcestershire sauce
- 1 teaspoon salt
- 1/2 teaspoon dried thyme
- 1/2 teaspoon pepper
- 2 bay leaves
- 1 meaty ham bone *or* 2 smoked ham hocks
- 1/4 cup minced fresh parsley

Place beans in a Dutch oven; add water to cover by 2 in. Bring to a boil; boil for 2 minutes. Remove from the heat; cover and let stand for 1 to 4 hours or until beans are softened. Drain and rinse beans, discarding liquid.

In the same pan, saute onions in oil for 2 minutes. Add celery; cook until tender. Stir in the beans, water, ham, potatoes, carrot, Worcestershire sauce, salt, thyme, pepper and bay leaves. Add ham bone. Bring to a boil. Reduce heat; cover and simmer for 1-1/4 to 1-1/2 hours or until beans are tender.

Discard bay leaves. Remove ham bone; and set aside until cool enough to handle. Remove ham from bone and cut into cubes. Discard bone. Return ham to soup; heat through. Garnish soup with parsley.

ham and bean soup

vegetable beef soup

PREP/TOTAL TIME: 30 min. | **YIELD:** 14 servings (3-1/2 quarts).

Brimming with veggies, this hearty soup will warm folks right to their toes! It's especially delicious served with corn bread, and it becomes even more thick and flavorful the next day.

MARIE CARLISLE, SUMRALL, MISSISSIPPI

4	cups cubed peeled potatoes
6	cups water
1	pound ground beef
5	teaspoons beef bouillon granules
1	can (10-3/4 ounces) condensed tomato soup, undiluted
2	cups frozen corn, thawed
2	cups frozen sliced carrots, thawed
2	cups frozen cut green beans, thawed
2	cups frozen sliced okra, thawed
3	tablespoons dried minced onion

In a Dutch oven, bring potatoes and water to a boil. Cover and cook for 10-15 minutes or until tender. Meanwhile, in a large skillet, cook beef over medium heat until no longer pink; drain.

Add the bouillon, soup, vegetables, dried minced onion and beef to the undrained potatoes. Bring to a boil. Reduce heat; simmer, uncovered, for 8-10 minutes or until heated through, stirring occasionally.

crawfish etouffee

PREP: 15 min. | **COOK:** 50 min. | **YIELD:** 6-8 servings.

I like to serve this Cajun sensation when I entertain. Etouffee is typically served with shellfish over rice and is similar to gumbo. The dish has its roots in New Orleans and the bayou country of Louisiana.

TAMRA DUNCAN, LINCOLN, ARKANSAS

1/2	cup butter, cubed
1/2	cup plus 2 tablespoons all-purpose flour
1-1/4	cups chopped celery
1	cup chopped green pepper
1/2	cup chopped green onions
1	can (14-1/2 ounces) chicken broth

1	cup water
1/4	cup minced fresh parsley
1	tablespoon tomato paste
1	bay leaf
1/2	teaspoon salt
1/4	teaspoon pepper
1/4	teaspoon cayenne pepper
2	pounds frozen cooked crawfish tail meat, thawed

Hot cooked rice

In a large heavy skillet, melt butter; stir in flour. Cook and stir over low heat for about 20 minutes until mixture is a caramel-colored paste. Add the celery, pepper and onions; stir until coated. Add the broth, water, parsley, tomato paste, bay leaf, salt, pepper and cayenne pepper. Bring to a boil.

Reduce heat; cover and simmer for 30 minutes, stirring occasionally. Discard bay leaf. Add crawfish and heat through. Serve with rice.

oyster stew

PREP: 15 min. | **COOK:** 30 min. | **YIELD:** 12 servings.

Rich and creamy oyster stew is a popular starter course for Thanksgiving in New Orleans. Serve it alongside turducken for a truly genuine Big Easy feast! CHRISTA SCOTT, SANTA FE, NEW MEXICO

3	medium leeks (white portion only), chopped
1/4	cup butter, cubed
2	medium potatoes, peeled and diced
2	cups hot water
3	teaspoons chicken bouillon granules
2	cups milk
2	cups half-and-half cream
4	cans (16 ounces *each*) oysters, drained
1/4	teaspoon cayenne pepper

Salt and pepper to taste

Minced fresh parsley

In a Dutch oven, saute leeks in butter for 10 minutes or until tender. Add the potatoes, water and bouillon; cover and simmer 20 minutes or until potatoes are tender. Cool.

Transfer to a blender. Cover and process until blended. Return to the pan; stir in the milk, cream, oysters, cayenne, salt and pepper. Cook on low until heated through (do not boil). Garnish with parsley.

cleaning leeks

Leeks often contain sand between their layers. Cut the leeks in half lengthwise. Rinse under cold running water, gently separating the leaves to allow the water to flush out any trapped sand or dirt.

brunswick stew

PREP: 1 hour + cooling | **COOK:** 45 min. | **YIELD:** 6 servings.

This thick stew is filled to the brim with a bounty of potatoes, lima beans, corn and tomatoes. Authentic versions call for rabbit or squirrel, but I think you'll like my recipe that uses tender chunks of chicken.
MILDRED SHERRER, FORT WORTH, TEXAS

1	broiler/fryer chicken (3-1/2 to 4 pounds), cut up
1	cup water
4	medium potatoes, peeled and cubed
2	medium onions, sliced
1	can (15-1/4 ounces) lima beans, rinsed and drained
1	teaspoon salt
1/2	teaspoon pepper

Dash cayenne pepper

1	can (15-1/4 ounces) corn, drained
1	can (14-1/2 ounces) diced tomatoes, undrained
1/4	cup butter
1/2	cup dry bread crumbs

In a Dutch oven, slowly bring the chicken and water to a boil. Cover and simmer for 45-60 minutes or until chicken is tender, skimming the surface as foam rises.

Remove chicken and set aside until cool enough to handle. Remove and discard skin and bones. Cube chicken and return to broth.

Add the potatoes, onions, beans and seasonings. Bring to a boil. Reduce heat; simmer, uncovered, for 30 minutes or until potatoes are tender. Stir in remaining ingredients. Simmer, uncovered, for 10 minutes or until slightly thickened.

brunswick stew

southwestern beef stew

PREP: 30 min. | **COOK:** 7-1/4 hours | **YIELD:** 7 servings.

This zippy stew seasoned with picante sauce is great on cold winter evenings. The preparation is so easy, it's ready in minutes after a busy day at work.

REGINA STOCK, TOPEKA, KANSAS

- 2 pounds beef stew meat, cut into 1-inch cubes
- 1 jar (16 ounces) picante sauce
- 2 medium potatoes, peeled and cut into 1/2-inch cubes
- 4 medium carrots, cut into 1/2-inch slices
- 1 large onion, chopped
- 1 teaspoon chili powder
- 1/4 teaspoon salt
- 1/4 teaspoon ground cumin
- 1 tablespoon cornstarch
- 1/4 cup cold water

In a large nonstick skillet coated with cooking spray, brown beef on all sides; drain. Transfer to a 3-qt. slow cooker. Stir in the picante sauce, potatoes, carrots, onion, chili powder, salt and cumin.

Cover and cook on low for 8-9 hours or until meat and vegetables are tender.

In a small bowl, combine cornstarch and water until smooth; stir into stew. Cover and cook on high for 15 minutes or until gravy is thickened.

southwestern beef stew

seafood gumbo

seafood gumbo

PREP: 20 min. | **COOK:** 30 min. | **YIELD:** about 6 quarts.

Gumbo is one of the dishes that helped make the Creole-Cajun cuisine of Louisiana so famous. We live across the border in Texas and can't get enough of this traditional Cajun version featuring okra, shrimp and spicy seasonings. This recipe calls for seafood, but you could also use chicken, duck or sausage.

RUTH AUBEY, SAN ANTONIO, TEXAS

- 1 cup all-purpose flour
- 1 cup canola oil
- 4 cups chopped onion
- 2 cups chopped celery
- 2 cups chopped green pepper
- 1 cup sliced green onion and tops
- 4 cups chicken broth
- 8 cups water
- 4 cups sliced okra
- 2 tablespoons paprika
- 2 tablespoons salt
- 2 teaspoons oregano
- 1 teaspoon ground black pepper
- 6 cups small shrimp, rinsed and drained, *or seafood of your choice*
- 1 cup minced fresh parsley
- 2 tablespoons Cajun seasoning

In a heavy Dutch oven, combine flour and oil until smooth. Cook over medium-high heat for 5 minutes, stirring constantly. Reduce heat to medium. Cook and stir about 10 minutes more, or until mixture is reddish-brown.

Add the onion, celery, green pepper and green onions; cook and stir for 5 minutes. Add the chicken broth, water, okra, paprika, salt, oregano and pepper. Bring to boil; reduce heat and simmer, covered, for 10 minutes.

Add shrimp and parsley. Simmer, uncovered, about 5 minutes more or until seafood is done. Remove from heat; stir in Cajun seasoning.

grandmother's chicken 'n' dumplings

PREP: 45 min. | **COOK:** 30 min. | **YIELD:** 8-10 servings.

When I was growing up, my grandmother could feed our entire family with a single chicken—and lots of dumplings. CATHY CARROLL, BOSSIER CITY, LOUISIANA

1	**large chicken (6 pounds)**
2	**teaspoons salt**
4	**quarts water**
2	**tablespoons white vinegar**
1	**large onion, sliced**
2	**medium carrots, chopped**
2	**celery ribs, sliced**

DUMPLINGS:

2	**cups all-purpose flour**
1-1/2	**teaspoons salt**
1	**egg**
1/2	**cup reserved chicken broth**

Pepper

Place the chicken, salt, water, vinegar, onion, carrots and celery in a large stockpot, adding more water, if necessary, to cover chicken. Bring to boil. Reduce heat; cover and simmer until meat nearly falls from the bones. Remove chicken from broth; allow to cool. Strain broth, discarding the vegetables and seasonings.

Remove meat from bones; discard skin and bones. Cut meat into bite-size pieces; set aside and keep warm. Set aside 1 cup broth; cool to lukewarm.

To make dumplings, combine flour and salt. Make a well in flour; add egg. Gradually stir 1/4 cup of reserved broth into egg, picking up flour as you go. Continue until flour is used up, adding additional broth as needed, and dough is consistency of pie dough. Pour any remaining reserved broth back into stockpot.

Turn dough onto floured surface; knead in additional flour to make stiff dough. Let dough rest for 15 minutes. On a floured surface, roll out the dough into a 17-in. square. Cut into 1-in. square pieces. Dust with additional flour; let dry for 30-60 minutes.

Bring broth to boil (you should have about 4 quarts). Drop squares into boiling broth. Reduce heat to a slow simmer; cover and simmer for 10 minutes. Uncover; cook until a until a toothpick inserted in a dumpling comes out clean (do not lift the cover while simmering). Dust with pepper and add reserved chicken meat.

summer strawberry soup

summer strawberry soup

PREP: 15 min. + chilling | **YIELD:** 6 servings.

You'll be amazed that just five ingredients can create something so spectacular! This fruity chilled soup is certain to become a new warm-weather favorite. VERNA BOLLIN, POWELL, TENNESSEE

2	**cups vanilla yogurt**
1/2	**cup orange juice**
2	**pounds fresh strawberries, halved (8 cups)**
1/2	**cup sugar**

Additional vanilla yogurt and fresh mint leaves, optional

In a blender, combine the yogurt, orange juice, strawberries and sugar in batches; cover and process until blended. Refrigerate for at least 2 hours. Garnish with additional yogurt and mint leaves if desired.

hulling strawberries

Use a strawberry huller or the tip of a serrated grapefruit spoon to easily remove the stem, or hull, of a strawberry. Just insert the tip of the spoon into the strawberry next to the hull and cut around it.

white bean chicken chili

white bean chicken chili

PREP: 35 min. | **COOK:** 3 hours | **YIELD:** 6 servings.

My sister shared this chili recipe with me. I usually double it and add one extra can of beans, then serve with cheddar biscuits or warmed tortillas. The jalapeno adds just the right amount of heat.
KRISTINE BOWLES, RIO RANCHO, NEW MEXICO

3/4	**pound boneless skinless chicken breasts, cubed**
1/2	**teaspoon salt**
1/4	**teaspoon pepper**
1	**medium onion, chopped**
1	**jalapeno pepper, seeded and chopped**
2	**teaspoons dried oregano**
1	**teaspoon ground cumin**
2	**tablespoons olive oil**
4	**garlic cloves, minced**
2	**cans (15 ounces *each*) white kidney *or* cannellini beans, rinsed and drained, *divided***
3	**cups chicken broth, *divided***
1-1/2	**cups (6 ounces) shredded cheddar cheese**

Sour cream and minced fresh cilantro, optional

Sprinkle chicken with salt and pepper. In a large skillet over medium heat, cook the chicken, onion, jalapeno, oregano and cumin in oil for 3-4 minutes or until chicken is browned and vegetables are crisp-tender. Add garlic; cook 1 minute longer.

Transfer to a 3-qt. slow cooker. In a small bowl, mash 1 cup of beans; add 1/2 cup broth and stir until blended. Add to the slow cooker with the remaining beans and broth. Cover and cook on low for 3 to 3-1/2 hours or until heated through.

Stir before serving. Sprinkle with cheese. Garnish with sour cream and cilantro if desired.

CHICKEN CORN CHILI: Add 2 cups thawed frozen corn and 1/2 teaspoon ground coriander to the slow cooker along with the broth. Proceed as directed.

EDITOR'S NOTE: We recommend wearing disposable gloves when cutting hot peppers. Avoid touching your face.

watermelon gazpacho

PREP/TOTAL TIME: 25 min. | **YIELD:** 4 servings.

This is a delightfully simple, elegant dish. Serve as a side or with pita and hummus for a meal. It's so refreshing. NICOLE DEELAH, NASHVILLE, TENNESSEE

4	**cups cubed watermelon, seeded, *divided***
2	**tablespoons lime juice**
1	**tablespoon grated lime peel**
1	**teaspoon minced fresh gingerroot**
1	**teaspoon salt**
1	**cup chopped tomato**
1/2	**cup chopped cucumber**
1/2	**cup chopped green pepper**
1/4	**cup minced fresh cilantro**
2	**tablespoons chopped green onion**
1	**tablespoon finely chopped seeded jalapeno pepper**

Puree 3 cups watermelon in a blender. Cut remaining watermelon into 1/2-inch pieces; set aside.

In a large bowl, combine the watermelon puree, lime juice, lime peel, ginger and salt. Stir in the tomato, cucumber, green pepper, cilantro, onion, jalapeno and cubed watermelon. Chill until serving.

EDITOR'S NOTE: We recommend wearing disposable gloves when cutting hot peppers. Avoid touching your face.

watermelon gazpacho

okra and butter bean stew

PREP: 25 min. | **COOK:** 45 min. | **YIELD:** 12 servings (1 cup each).

I adapted this stew from my mom's down-home Louisiana recipe. I guarantee it will turns okra haters into okra lovers. KAYA MACK, WICHITA FALLS, TEXAS

- 7 **bacon strips, chopped**
- 1 **pound smoked sausage, halved and thinly sliced**
- 1 **large onion, chopped**
- 2 **small green peppers, chopped**
- 3 **cups water**
- 2 **cans (16 ounces *each*) butter beans, rinsed and drained**
- 1 **can (14-1/2 ounces) diced tomatoes, undrained**
- 1 **can (12 ounces) tomato paste**
- 1 **teaspoon pepper**
- 1/4 **teaspoon salt**
- 1 **package (16 ounces) frozen sliced okra**

Hot cooked rice, optional

In a Dutch oven, cook bacon and sausage over medium heat until bacon is crisp. Remove to paper towels; drain, reserving 2 tablespoons drippings.

Cook onion and green peppers in the drippings until tender. Stir in the water, beans, tomatoes, tomato paste, pepper and salt. Bring to a boil. Reduce heat; simmer, uncovered, for 10 minutes. Add bacon and sausage; cook 10 minutes longer.

Stir in okra. Cover and cook for 8-10 minutes or until okra is tender. Serve with rice if desired.

okra defined

Okra is a vegetable that is popular in the southern United States, where it is often added to soups and stews. It has grayish-green ridged pods that contain numerous small edible seeds. When okra is sliced, it releases a substance that naturally thickens any liquid it is cooked in.

shrimp and black bean soup

PREP: 20 min. | **COOK:** 40 min. | **YIELD:** 8 servings (3 quarts).

My bold and spicy soup is packed with tomatoes, black beans, corn and, of course, shrimp! My family enjoys foods that have a little zip, and this chunky sensation fills the bill.

ELIZABETH LEWIS, HAYDEN, ALABAMA

1	large onion, chopped
1	tablespoon olive oil
2	cans (14-1/2 ounces *each*) reduced-sodium chicken broth
2	cans (10 ounces *each*) diced tomatoes and green chilies, undrained
2	cups frozen corn
1	can (15 ounces) black beans, rinsed and drained
1	can (14-1/2 ounces) diced tomatoes, undrained
4-1/2	teaspoons chili powder
1	teaspoon sugar
1/2	teaspoon salt
1	pound uncooked medium shrimp, peeled and deveined
1/4	cup minced fresh parsley

In a Dutch oven, saute onion in oil for 3-4 minutes or until tender. Add the broth, tomatoes and green chilies, corn, black beans, tomatoes, chili powder, sugar and salt. Bring to a boil, stirring occasionally. Reduce heat; cover and simmer for 20 minutes.

Stir in shrimp; cook 5-6 minutes longer or until shrimp turn pink. Stir in parsley.

creole jambalaya

PREP: 20 min. | **COOK:** 35 min. | **YIELD:** 8 servings.

Creole jambalaya, also known as red jambalaya, is a traditional Louisiana dish with deep roots in French and Spanish cuisines. Tomatoes, seafood, rice, and the holy trinity of onions, green peppers and celery are the key ingredients in this Southern favorite. Most recipes also call for chicken or sausage, but mine uses ham for a unique taste twist.

RUBY WILLIAMS, BOGALUSA, LOUISIANA

3/4	cup chopped onion
1/2	cup chopped celery
1/4	cup chopped green pepper
2	tablespoons butter
2	garlic cloves, minced
2	cups cubed fully cooked ham
1	can (28 ounces) diced tomatoes, undrained
1	can (10-1/2 ounces) condensed beef broth, undiluted

shrimp and black bean soup

1	cup uncooked long grain white rice
1	cup water
1	teaspoon sugar
1	teaspoon dried thyme
1/2	teaspoon chili powder
1/4	teaspoon pepper
1-1/2	pounds fresh *or* frozen uncooked shrimp, peeled and deveined
1	tablespoon minced fresh parsley

In a Dutch oven, saute the onion, celery and green pepper in butter until tender. Add garlic; cook 1 minute longer. Add the next nine ingredients; bring to a boil. Reduce heat; cover and simmer until rice is tender, about 25 minutes.

Add shrimp and parsley; simmer, uncovered, for 7-10 minutes or until shrimp turn pink.

crab corn chowder

PREP/TOTAL TIME: 25 min. | **YIELD:** 8 servings.

No time to make a homemade soup? Think again! This hearty chowder features a rich, creamy broth that's brimming with chunks of crab and crunchy corn. You'll be ladling out steamy bowls in no time. It's one of the best I've ever tasted.

SARAH MCCLANAHAN, RALEIGH, NORTH CAROLINA

3	teaspoons chicken bouillon granules
2	cups boiling water
6	bacon strips, diced
1/3	cup *each* diced sweet red, yellow and orange peppers
1/2	cup chopped onion
1/4	cup all-purpose flour
3	cups half-and-half cream
2	cans (14-3/4 ounces *each*) cream-style corn
1-1/2	teaspoons seasoned salt
1/2	teaspoon dried basil
1/4	to 1/2 teaspoon cayenne pepper
2	cans (6 ounces *each*) crabmeat, drained, flaked and cartilage removed *or* 2 cups imitation crabmeat, flaked
1/2	cup minced chives

Dissolve bouillon in water; set aside. In a Dutch oven, cook bacon over medium heat until crisp. Remove bacon to paper towels to drain, reserving drippings.

In the same pan, saute peppers and onion in drippings until tender. Stir in flour. Gradually stir in bouillon. Bring to a boil; cook and stir for 2 minutes or until thickened.

Reduce the heat; gradually stir in cream and corn. Add the seasoned salt, basil and cayenne. Cook for 8-10 minutes or until heated through, stirring occasionally (do not boil). Stir in the crab. Garnish each bowl with bacon and chives.

truly texan chili

truly texan chili

PREP: 10 min. | **COOK:** 1-3/4 hours | **YIELD:** 4-6 servings (5 cups).

I am a native Texan, and this is the best chili recipe I've ever tasted. It's meaty and spicy. I'd make this whenever I was homesick during the years we spent away from Texas due to my husband's military career.

BETTY BROWN, SAN ANTONIO, TEXAS

3	pounds ground beef
2	to 3 garlic cloves, minced
3	tablespoons chili powder (or to taste)
1	tablespoon ground cumin
1/4	cup all-purpose flour
1	tablespoon dried oregano
2	cans (14-1/2 ounces *each*) beef broth
1	teaspoon salt
1/4	teaspoon pepper
1	can (15 ounces) pinto beans, rinsed and drained, optional

Optional garnishes: shredded cheddar cheese, tortilla chips, sour cream *and/or* lime wedges

In a Dutch oven, cook beef over medium heat until no longer pink; drain. Reduce heat; stir in garlic. Combine the chili powder, cumin, flour and oregano; sprinkle over meat, stirring until evenly coated. Add the broth, salt and pepper; bring to a boil, stirring occasionally.

Reduce heat; cover and simmer for 1-1/2 to 2 hours, stirring occasionally. (Chili can be transferred to a slow cooker for simmering if desired.)

Cool. Cover and refrigerate overnight. Reheat in a Dutch oven or 3-qt. slow cooker over low heat. If desired, add beans and heat through. Garnish individual bowls if desired with cheese, tortilla chips, sour cream and/or lime wedges.

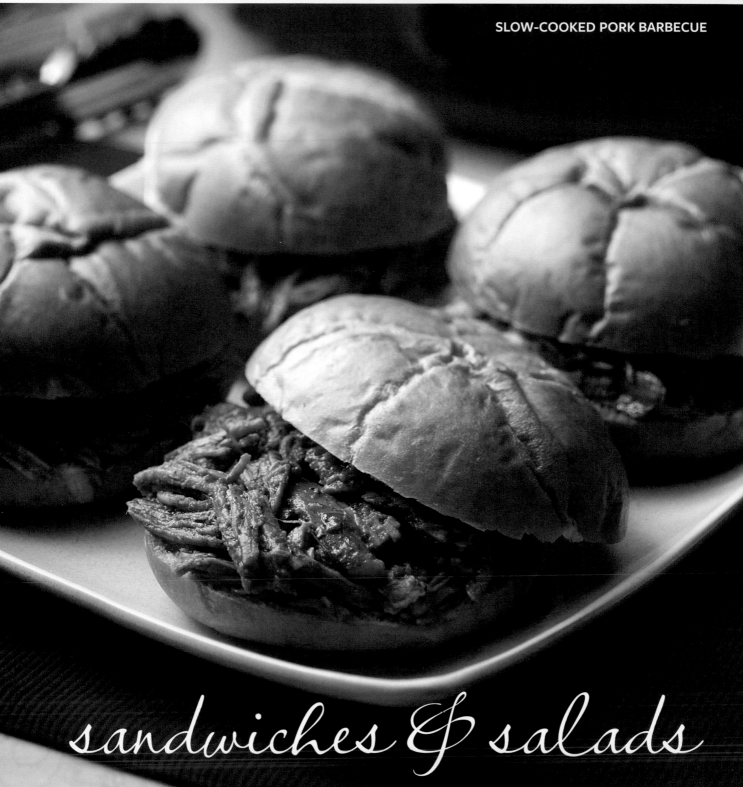

SLOW-COOKED PORK BARBECUE

sandwiches & salads

slow-cooked pork barbecue

PREP: 15 min. | **COOK:** 5 hours | **YIELD:** 10 servings.

You need only five ingredients to fix this sweet and tender pork for sandwiches. I think it's perfect just the way it is, but feel free to adjust the sauce ingredients to suit your family's tastes.
CONNIE JOHNSON, SPRINGFIELD, MISSOURI

1	boneless pork loin roast (3 to 4 pounds)
1-1/2	teaspoons seasoned salt
1	teaspoon garlic powder
1	cup barbecue sauce
1	cup cola
10	sandwich buns, split

Cut roast in half; place in a 5-qt. slow cooker. Sprinkle with seasoned salt and garlic powder. Cover and cook on low for 4-5 hours or until meat is tender.

Remove meat; skim fat from cooking juices. Shred meat with two forks and return to the slow cooker. Combine barbecue sauce and cola; pour over meat. Cover and cook on high for 1-2 hours or until sauce is thickened. Serve on rolls.

corn bread layered salad

PREP: 20 min. | **BAKE:** 20 min. + cooling | **YIELD:** 6-8 servings.

My mom's layered corn bread salad is so filling, it's a meal in itself! It's a great for picnics and potlucks.
JODY MILLER, OKLAHOMA CITY, OKLAHOMA

1	package (8-1/2 ounces) corn bread/muffin mix
6	green onions, chopped
1	medium green pepper, chopped
1	can (15-1/4 ounces) whole kernel corn, drained
1	can (15 ounces) pinto beans, rinsed and drained
3/4	cup mayonnaise
3/4	cup sour cream
2	medium tomatoes, seeded and chopped
1/2	cup shredded cheddar cheese

Prepare and bake corn bread according to package directions. Cool on a wire rack.

homemade corn bread

It's easy to make your own homemade corn bread. In a large bowl, combine 1 cup flour, 1 cup yellow cornmeal, 1/4 cup sugar, 2 teaspoons baking powder and 3/4 teaspoon salt. Add two lightly beaten eggs, 1 cup milk and 1/4 cup canola oil. Beat just until moistened. Spoon into a greased 8-in. square baking pan. Bake at 400° for 20-25 minutes or until a toothpick inserted in the center comes out clean.

Crumble corn bread into a 2-qt. glass serving bowl. Layer with onions, green pepper, corn and beans.

In a small bowl, combine mayonnaise and sour cream; spread over the vegetables. Sprinkle with tomatoes and cheese. Refrigerate until serving.

black-eyed pea salad

PREP/TOTAL TIME: 10 min. | **YIELD:** 4 servings.

I've had lots of compliments and requests for this recipe over the years. My husband loves it, and it's especially great on hot days. The Italian salad dressing keeps the avocado from turning dark so it's great for buffet tables, and it makes a fun alternative to typical pasta or potato salads.
NANCY CARIKER, BAKERSFIELD, CALIFORNIA

1	can (15-1/2 ounces) black-eyed peas, rinsed and drained
1	large tomato, diced
1	medium ripe avocado, peeled and diced
1/3	cup chopped green pepper
2	green onions, chopped
1	tablespoon minced fresh cilantro
1	jalapeno pepper, seeded and chopped
1/3	cup Italian salad dressing

In a large serving bowl, combine all the ingredients; toss to coat. Serve with a slotted spoon.

BLACK-EYED PEA CORN SALAD: Omit the tomato, avocado, green pepper and green onions. Add 2 cups corn and 1/4 cup chopped red onion to the salad mixture.

EDITOR'S NOTE: We recommend wearing disposable gloves when cutting hot peppers. Avoid touching your face.

black-eyed pea salad

raspberry congealed salad

5-1/2 cups coleslaw mix
1/2 cup heavy whipping cream
1/3 cup sugar
3 tablespoons white vinegar
1/2 teaspoon salt

Place coleslaw mix in a serving bowl. In a small bowl, combine the remaining ingredients. Pour over coleslaw mix and toss to coat. Chill until serving.

fire and ice tomatoes

PREP: 10 min. + chilling | **YIELD:** 8 servings.

You won't miss the salt in this cool tomato salad. It's well-seasoned with cayenne pepper, mustard seed and vinegar, but not the least bit spicy.

NAN RICKEY, YUMA, ARIZONA

5 large tomatoes, cut into wedges
1 medium onion, sliced
3/4 cup white vinegar
6 tablespoons sugar
1/4 cup water
1 tablespoon mustard seed
1/4 teaspoon cayenne pepper
1 large cucumber, sliced

In a large bowl, combine the tomatoes and onion; set aside. In a small saucepan, combine the vinegar, sugar, water, mustard seed and cayenne. Bring to a boil; boil for 1 minute.

Pour over tomatoes and onion; toss to coat. Cover and refrigerate for at least 2 hours. Add cucumber; toss to coat. Refrigerate overnight. Serve with a slotted spoon.

raspberry congealed salad

PREP: 20 min. + chilling | **YIELD:** 6 servings.

A Southern meal isn't complete without a refreshing congealed salad on the side. My sisters and I especially enjoy our Mom's tangy, ruby-red delight. The pineapple and raspberries are a delectable duo, and pecans add a pleasant crunch.

NANCY DUTY, JACKSONVILLE, FLORIDA

1 can (8 ounces) crushed pineapple
1 package (12 ounces) frozen unsweetened raspberries, thawed
1 package (3 ounces) raspberry gelatin
1 cup applesauce
1/4 cup coarsely chopped pecans
Mayonnaise, optional

Drain pineapple and raspberries, reserving juices. Place fruit in a large bowl; set aside. Add enough water to the juice to measure 1 cup. Pour into a saucepan; bring to a boil. Remove from the heat; stir in gelatin until dissolved.

Pour over fruit mixture. Add the applesauce and pecans. Pour into a 1-qt. bowl. Chill until set. Spoon into individual dessert dishes; top with a dollop of mayonnaise if desired.

sweet 'n' sour coleslaw

PREP/TOTAL TIME: 5 min. | **YIELD:** 4 servings.

My coleslaw comes together in just 5 minutes and brings bright flavor and crunch to the menu. This was my mother's recipe, and I'm always asked to share it.

BARBARA KEITH, FAUCETT, MISSOURI

fire and ice tomatoes

hot brown sandwiches

PREP/TOTAL TIME: 25 min. | **YIELD:** 8 servings.

Hot browns are a local favorite in Louisville and all throughout Kentucky. In 1926, Fred Schmidt, a chef at the famous Brown Hotel, invented the sandwich to serve guests at the hotel's late-night soirees. He believed they deserved something more special than standard ham and eggs, and subsequently the open-faced creation became a legend!

TASTE OF HOME TEST KITCHEN

1/4	cup butter
1/4	cup all-purpose flour
1	cup milk
1	cup chicken broth
1/2	teaspoon Worcestershire sauce
3/4	cup shredded cheddar cheese
1/4	teaspoon salt
1/8	teaspoon white pepper
8	slices Italian bread (1/2 inch thick), toasted
1-1/2	pounds sliced cooked turkey
8	cooked bacon strips, halved
2	medium tomatoes, sliced
1	cup (4 ounces) shredded Parmesan cheese

In a large saucepan, melt butter over low heat. Stir in flour until smooth; gradually add milk, broth and Worcestershire sauce. Bring to a boil; cook and stir for 2 minutes or until thickened. Stir in the cheese, salt and white pepper until cheese is melted. Remove from the heat.

Place slices of toast on a baking sheet. Layer each with turkey, cheese sauce, bacon, tomatoes and Parmesan cheese. Broil 3-4 in. from the heat for 3-4 minutes or until cheese is melted.

shrimp 'n' slaw puffs

PREP/TOTAL TIME: 15 min. | **YIELD:** 4 servings.

Coleslaw mix and bottled dressing cut the prep time for this colorful and delicious sandwich filling to practically nothing! That leaves you with more time to set a pretty luncheon table and visit with guests.
TASTE OF HOME TEST KITCHEN

1/2	pound cooked small shrimp, peeled and deveined and chopped
2	cups coleslaw mix
2	tablespoons chopped green onion
2	tablespoons chopped sweet yellow pepper
1/4	cup coleslaw salad dressing
1	tablespoon capers, drained and patted dry
1	teaspoon snipped fresh dill *or* 1/4 teaspoon dill weed
1/4	teaspoon salt
1/4	teaspoon pepper
4	cream puff shells

In a large bowl, combine the shrimp, coleslaw mix, onion and yellow pepper. In a small bowl, combine the coleslaw dressing, capers, dill, salt and pepper. Pour over shrimp mixture and gently toss to coat.

Refrigerate until serving. Just before serving, spoon 1/2 cup shrimp salad into each cream puff; replace tops.

shrimp 'n' slaw puffs

avocado chicken salad

avocado chicken salad

PREP/TOTAL TIME: 20 min. | **YIELD:** 5 servings.

My family requests I bring this flavorful chicken salad to all of our parties and reunions. I sometimes serve it in pita bread for a filling grab-and-go lunch.
KARLENE JOHNSON, MOORESVILLE, NORTH CAROLINA

1	medium ripe avocado, peeled and cubed
2	tablespoons lemon juice, *divided*
2	cups cubed cooked chicken
2	cups seedless red grapes, halved
1	medium tart apple, chopped
1	cup chopped celery
3/4	cup mayonnaise
1/2	cup chopped walnuts, toasted
1/2	teaspoon ground ginger

Lettuce leaves, optional

In a small bowl, toss avocado with 1 tablespoon lemon juice; set aside. In a large bowl, combine the chicken, grapes, apple, celery, mayonnaise, walnuts, ginger and remaining lemon juice. Stir in avocado. Serve on lettuce-lined plates if desired.

honey poppy seed dressing

PREP/TOTAL TIME: 5 min. | **YIELD:** 3/4 cup.

This sweet dressing is a favorite at our house. I toss it on all of our garden salads because the flavor blends so well with fresh greens and vegetables. I enjoy sharing the recipe with others, too, and have received many compliments on it.
ABIGAIL STAUFFER, PORT TREVORTON, PENNSYLVANIA

1/3	cup canola oil
1/4	cup honey
2	tablespoons cider vinegar
2	teaspoons poppy seeds
1/2	teaspoon salt
Fresh fruit *or* **mixed greens**	

In a jar with a tight-fitting lid, combine the first five ingredients. Cover and shake well. Store in the refrigerator until serving. Serve with fruit or mixed greens.

next-generation german potato salad

PREP/TOTAL TIME: 30 min. | **YIELD:** 14 servings.

You'd be surprised how popular German-style potato salad is in Oklahoma and other parts of the Southwest. Balsamic vinegar and bacon infuse it with a unique taste twist.
MARY SHIVERS, ADA, OKLAHOMA

4	pounds small red potatoes, quartered
10	bacon strips, chopped
1	large onion, chopped
3	tablespoons chopped celery
2	tablespoons chopped green pepper
1	tablespoon all-purpose flour
1	tablespoon sugar
1	teaspoon salt
1/2	teaspoon pepper
1	cup water
1/3	cup white balsamic vinegar

Place the potatoes in a Dutch oven and cover with water. Bring to a boil. Reduce heat; cover and simmer for 15-20 minutes or until tender.

next-generation german potato salad

egg salad sandwiches

Meanwhile, in a large skillet, cook bacon over medium heat until crisp. Using a slotted spoon, remove to paper towels. In the drippings, saute the onion, celery and green pepper until tender. Stir in the flour, sugar, salt and pepper until blended. Combine water and vinegar; stir into vegetable mixture. Bring to a boil; cook and stir for 2 minutes or until thickened.

Drain potatoes and place in a large serving bowl. Pour dressing over potatoes. Add bacon and toss to coat. Serve warm or at room temperature. Refrigerate leftovers.

egg salad sandwiches

PREP/TOTAL TIME: 15 min. | **YIELD:** 6 servings.

The ingredients in this sandwich are simple, yet each one accentuates the flavor, making it hard to stop with just one bite!
ANNA JEAN ALLEN, WEST LIBERTY, KENTUCKY

1	cup (4 ounces) shredded cheddar cheese
1/2	cup chopped green pepper
1/2	cup sweet pickles, chopped
1/4	cup mayonnaise
2	tablespoons horseradish sauce
1	tablespoon sweet pickle juice
1/4	teaspoon salt
6	hard-cooked eggs, chopped
12	slices white bread
Lettuce leaves and tomato slices, optional	

In a small bowl, combine the first seven ingredients; stir in the eggs.

On six slices of bread, layer with 1/2 cup egg salad, lettuce and tomato slices if desired. Top with remaining bread slices.

potato salad

PREP: 30 min. + chilling | **YIELD:** 6 servings.

With creamy chunks of potatoes and sliced hard-cooked eggs on top, this treasured Southern favorite will elicit rave reviews from your gang.

DOROTHY BAYES, SARDIS, OHIO

4	**cups cubed peeled potatoes**
1	**celery rib, thinly sliced**
1/3	**cup finely chopped onion**
1/3	**cup sweet pickle relish**
3/4	**cup fat-free mayonnaise**
1	**teaspoon ground mustard**
1/2	**teaspoon salt**
1/4	**teaspoon celery seed**
1/8	**teaspoon pepper**
2	**hard-cooked eggs, sliced**
1/8	**teaspoon paprika**

Place potatoes in a large saucepan and cover with water. Bring to a boil. Reduce heat; cover and simmer for 10-15 minutes or until tender. Drain and cool to room temperature.

In a large bowl, combine the potatoes, celery, onion and relish. In a small bowl, combine the mayonnaise, mustard, salt, celery seed and pepper. Pour over potato mixture and toss to coat.

Cover and refrigerate until chilled. Top with eggs and sprinkle with paprika.

potato salad shortcut

To save time when preparing potato salad, place the peeled cooked potatoes and peeled hard-cooked eggs into a bowl and use a pastry blender to chop them instead of chopping each one individually by hand.

shrimp po' boys

PREP: 30 min. | **COOK:** 15 min. | **YIELD:** 8 servings.

Whether you're rich or poor, you'll feel like a million bucks after one big bite into these Louisiana-style submarine sandwiches. Adjust the amount of cayenne pepper to suit your tastes.
BETTY JEAN JORDAN, MONTICELLO, GEORGIA

1/2	cup mayonnaise
1/2	cup finely chopped onion
1/2	cup chopped dill pickles
1-1/3	cups all-purpose flour
1	teaspoon salt
4	eggs, *separated*
1-1/3	cups milk
2	tablespoons canola oil
8	French sandwich rolls, split

Additional oil for deep-fat frying

2	pounds uncooked large shrimp, peeled and deveined

Cayenne pepper to taste

4	cups shredded lettuce
16	tomato slices

In a small bowl, combine the mayonnaise, onion and pickles; set aside. For batter, combine flour and salt in a bowl. Add the egg yolks, milk and oil; beat until smooth.

In a small bowl, beat the egg whites until stiff peaks form; fold in batter.

Wrap sandwich rolls in foil. Bake at 350° for 10 minutes or until warmed. Meanwhile, in a large skillet or deep-fat fryer,

club sandwiches

heat 1/2 in. of oil to 375°. Dip shrimp in batter; fry for 2-3 minutes on each side or until golden brown. Drain on paper towels; sprinkle with cayenne

Spread mayonnaise mixture over rolls; top with lettuce, tomato slices and shrimp.

club sandwiches

PREP/TOTAL TIME: 25 min. | **YIELD:** 4 servings.

I'm a busy wife, mother, grandmother and great-grandmother. One of my family's lunch favorites is this layered creation that we call "hunka munka." It's a masterpiece of a sandwich and hearty enough to be a complete meal. JANET MILLER, MIDLAND, TEXAS

1/2	cup mayonnaise
4	French rolls, split
1	cup shredded lettuce
8	slices tomato
1	medium ripe avocado, peeled and sliced
1/4	cup prepared Italian salad dressing
1/2	teaspoon coarsely ground pepper
12	cooked bacon strips
1/2	pound sliced deli turkey
1/2	pound sliced deli ham
4	slices Swiss cheese

Spread mayonnaise over cut sides of rolls. On roll bottoms, layer the lettuce, tomato and avocado. Drizzle with dressing; sprinkle with pepper. Layer with bacon, turkey, ham and cheese. Replace roll tops.

shrimp po' boys

cajun catfish sandwiches

PREP/TOTAL TIME: 25 min. | **YIELD:** 4 servings.

My spicy, bistro-style sandwich makes a no-fuss summertime supper. Serve alongside any vegetable side dish for a complete meal.

SHAUNIECE FRAZIER, LOS ANGELES, CALIFORNIA

3/4	teaspoon seasoned pepper
1/2	teaspoon chili powder
1/2	teaspoon cayenne pepper
1/4	teaspoon seasoned salt
4	catfish fillets (4 ounces *each*)
2	teaspoons olive oil, *divided*
2	green onions, chopped
3	garlic cloves, minced
1/2	cup fat-free mayonnaise
4	French *or* kaiser rolls, split and toasted
4	romaine leaves

Combine the seasoned pepper, chili powder, cayenne and seasoned salt; sprinkle over fillets. In a large skillet, cook fillets in 1 teaspoon oil for 4-6 minutes on each side or until fish flakes easily with a fork. Remove and keep warm.

In the same skillet, saute onions in remaining oil until onions are tender. Add garlic; cook 1 minute longer. Remove from the heat; stir in mayonnaise. Spread over rolls; top each with a romaine leaf and fillet. Replace tops.

cajun catfish sandwiches

ambrosia fruit salad

ambrosia fruit salad

PREP/TOTAL TIME: 10 min. | **YIELD:** 6 servings.

This fresh and creamy salad is a favorite around our house. I make it with plenty of healthy fruit and yogurt and a generous helping of "goodies" (marshmallows and coconut), so it tastes like the rich version I grew up with.

TRISHA KRUSE, EAGLE, IDAHO

1	can (8-1/4 ounces) fruit cocktail, drained
1	can (8 ounces) unsweetened pineapple chunks, drained
1	cup green grapes
1	cup seedless red grapes
1	cup miniature marshmallows
1	medium banana, sliced
3/4	cup vanilla yogurt
1/2	cup flaked coconut

In a large bowl, combine all the ingredients.

avocado salad dressing

PREP/TOTAL TIME: 10 min. | **YIELD:** 2 cups.

Avocado, parsley and dill add freshness, flavor and a lovely color to this creamy and delicious dressing, making it an easy choice for a picnic pasta salad.

TASTE OF HOME TEST KITCHEN

1	cup buttermilk
1/2	cup fat-free plain yogurt
1	ripe avocado, peeled and sliced
2	green onions, chopped
1/4	cup minced fresh parsley
1/2	teaspoon salt
1/2	teaspoon garlic powder
1/4	teaspoon dill weed
1/8	teaspoon pepper

In a blender, combine all ingredients; cover and process until blended. Transfer to a jar with a tight-fitting lid or small bowl. Serve immediately or refrigerate.

watermelon and tomato salad

PREP: 40 min. | **YIELD:** 12 servings.

Nothing beats this light and refreshing medley on a hot day. The combination of watermelon, cilantro, lime and tasty heirloom tomatoes is unique enough to keep folks commenting on the great flavor—and coming back for more!

BEV JONES, BRUNSWICK, MISSOURI

3	tablespoons lime juice
2	tablespoons white balsamic vinegar
2	tablespoons olive oil
2	tablespoons honey
1	medium mango, peeled and chopped
1	teaspoon grated lime peel
1	teaspoon kosher salt
1/4	teaspoon white pepper
8	cups cubed seedless watermelon
1-1/2	pounds yellow tomatoes, coarsely chopped (about 5 medium)
1-1/2	pounds red tomatoes, coarsely chopped (about 5 medium)
2	sweet onions, thinly sliced and separated into rings
2/3	cup minced fresh cilantro

For dressing, place the first eight ingredients in a blender; cover and process until pureed.

In a large bowl, combine the watermelon, tomatoes, onions and cilantro. Just before serving, add dressing and toss to coat. Serve with a slotted spoon.

watermelon and tomato salad

italian muffuletta

PREP/TOTAL TIME: 25 min. | **YIELD:** 6 servings.

Muffuletta sounds Italian and, made with Italian meats piled high on a large round Sicilian bread, it tastes Italian, too. But its roots are Southern as it originated in the early 1900s in New Orleans when Salvatore Lupo, a Sicilian immigrant, created the signature sandwich to serve the patrons of his grocery store in the heart of the French Quarter.

DANA SCHMITT, AMES, IOWA

2/3	cup pimiento-stuffed olives, chopped
1	can (4-1/4 ounces) chopped ripe olives
6	tablespoons shredded Parmesan cheese
1/4	cup Italian salad dressing
2	teaspoons minced garlic
1	round loaf (1 pound) unsliced Italian bread
1/2	pound sliced deli turkey
1/4	pound sliced Swiss cheese
1/4	pound thinly sliced hard salami
1/4	pound sliced provolone cheese
1/4	pound thinly sliced bologna

In a small bowl, combine the first five ingredients; set aside.

Cut bread in half horizontally; hollow out top and bottom, leaving a 1-in. shell (save removed bread for another use).

Spoon half of the olive mixture on bottom half of bread. Layer with turkey, Swiss cheese, salami, provolone cheese, bologna and remaining olive mixture. Replace bread top. Cut into six wedges.

48

49

50

52

BARBECUED BEANS

side dishes & condiments

barbecued beans

PREP: 5 min. + standing | **COOK:** 10 hours | **YIELD:** 12-15 servings.

Most members of my family would agree that no picnic is complete until these delicious beans make their grand appearance on the buffet table. Preparing them in a slow cooker makes them easy to transport to any gathering, big or small.
DIANE HIXON, NICEVILLE, FLORIDA

- 1 pound dried navy beans
- 1 pound bacon strips, cooked and crumbled
- 1 bottle (32 ounces) tomato juice
- 1 can (8 ounces) tomato sauce
- 2 cups chopped onions
- 2/3 cup packed brown sugar
- 1 tablespoon soy sauce
- 2 teaspoons garlic salt
- 1 teaspoon ground mustard
- 1 teaspoon Worcestershire sauce

Place beans in a large saucepan; add water to cover by 2 in. Bring to a boil; boil for 2 minutes. Remove from the heat; let stand for 1 hour. Drain beans and discard liquid.

In a 5-qt. slow cooker, combine remaining ingredients. Add the beans. Cover and cook on high for 2 hours. Reduce heat to low and cook 8-10 hours longer or until beans are tender.

cheese 'n' grits casserole

PREP: 10 min. | **BAKE:** 30 min. + standing | **YIELD:** 8 servings.

Grits are a staple in Southern cooking, and this hearty casserole is always a crowd-pleaser. Serve this as a brunch item with bacon or as a side dish for dinner. JENNIFER WALLIS, GOLDSBORO, NORTH CAROLINA

- 4 cups water
- 1 cup uncooked old-fashioned grits
- 1/2 teaspoon salt
- 1/2 cup 2% milk
- 1/4 cup butter, melted
- 2 eggs, lightly beaten
- 1 cup (4 ounces) shredded cheddar cheese
- 1 tablespoon Worcestershire sauce
- 1/8 teaspoon cayenne pepper
- 1/8 teaspoon paprika

In a large saucepan, bring water to a boil. Slowly stir in grits and salt. Reduce heat; cover and simmer for 5-7 minutes or until thickened. Cool slightly. Gradually whisk in milk, butter and eggs. Stir in cheese, Worcestershire sauce and cayenne.

Transfer to a greased 2-qt. baking dish. Sprinkle with paprika. Bake, uncovered, at 350° for 30-35 minutes or until bubbly. Let stand 10 minutes before serving.

tomato 'n' corn risotto

PREP: 15 min. | **COOK:** 35 min. | **YIELD:** 5 servings.

This is one of my favorite recipes because it uses items from the garden. Milk and Parmesan cheese give it a creaminess everyone is sure to enjoy.
ANGELA LIVELY, BAXTER, TENNESSEE

- 2-1/2 cups water
- 2 cups whole milk
- 3 tablespoons chicken broth
- 1 large onion, finely chopped
- 2 tablespoons butter
- 1 garlic clove, minced
- 3/4 cup uncooked arborio rice
- 1-1/3 cups fresh corn (about 5 ears of corn)
- 1 medium tomato, peeled, seeded and chopped
- 1/2 cup grated Parmesan cheese
- 1/2 cup fresh basil leaves, thinly sliced
- 1/2 teaspoon salt

Pepper to taste

In a large saucepan, heat the water, milk and broth; keep warm.

In a large skillet, saute onion in butter until tender. Add garlic; cook 1 minute longer. Add rice; cook and stir for 2-3 minutes. Stir in 1 cup hot water mixture. Cook and stir until all liquid is absorbed.

Add remaining water mixture, 1/2 cup at a time, stirring constantly. Allow the liquid to absorb between additions. Cook until risotto is creamy and rice is almost tender. (Cooking time is about 20 minutes.) Stir in the remaining ingredients; heat through.

tomato 'n' corn risotto

bread and butter pickles

PREP: 30 min. | **PROCESS:** 15 min. | **YIELD:** 7 pints.

My mom always made these crisp pickles when we were kids, and she gave me the recipe. They are pleasantly tart and so good.
KAREN OWEN, RISING SUN, INDIANA

4	pounds cucumbers, sliced
8	small onions, sliced
1/2	cup canning salt
5	cups sugar
4	cups white vinegar
2	tablespoons mustard seed
2	teaspoons celery seed
1-1/2	teaspoons ground turmeric
1/2	teaspoon ground cloves

In a large container, combine the cucumbers, onions and salt. Cover with crushed ice and mix well. Let stand for 3 hours. drain; rinse and drain again.

In a Dutch oven, combine the sugar, vinegar and seasonings; bring to a boil. Add cucumber mixture; return to a boil. Remove from the heat.

Carefully ladle hot mixture into hot pint jars, leaving 1/2-in. headspace. Remove air bubbles, wipe rims and adjust lids. Process for 15 minutes in a boiling-water canner.

EDITOR'S NOTE: The processing time listed is for altitudes of 1,000 feet or less. For altitudes up to 3,000 feet, add 5 minutes; 6,000 feet, add 10 minutes; 8,000 feet, add 15 minutes; 10,000 feet, add 20 minutes.

mexicorn grits

PREP: 20 min. | **BAKE:** 35 min. | **YIELD:** 10 servings.

I grew up on grits and have fixed them in various ways. I decided to give them a new twist with this recipe. Even the leftovers are good.
BARBARA MOORHEAD, GAFFNEY, SOUTH CAROLINA

4	cups milk
1/2	cup plus 1/3 cup butter, *divided*
1	cup quick-cooking grits
2	eggs
1	can (11 ounces) Mexicorn, drained
1	can (4 ounces) chopped green chilies
1	cup (4 ounces) shredded Mexican cheese blend
1	teaspoon salt
1/4	teaspoon white pepper
1	cup shredded Parmesan cheese

In a large saucepan, bring milk and 1/2 cup butter to a boil. Slowly stir in grits. Reduce heat; cook and stir for 5-7 minutes.

In a small bowl, whisk the eggs. Stir a small amount of hot grits into eggs; return all to the pan, stirring constantly. Melt remaining butter; stir into grits. Add the corn, chilies, cheese, salt and pepper.

Transfer to a greased 2-qt. baking dish. Sprinkle with Parmesan cheese. Bake, uncovered, at 350° for 35-40 minutes or until a knife inserted near the center comes out clean.

bread and butter pickles

fried green tomatoes

PREP: 20 min. | **COOK:** 25 min. | **YIELD:** 10 servings.

Fried green tomatoes are a great way to make use of the end-of-the-season crop. Panko bread crumbs lend a uniquely light and crispy texture. You can also use this recipe with red tomatoes if you prefer, but make sure they are firm. Enjoy this Southern favorite on a summer evening while sipping a glass of sweet tea.

JACQUELYNNE STINE, LAS VEGAS, NEVADA

- 3/4 **cup all-purpose flour**
- 3 **eggs, lightly beaten**
- 2 **cups panko (Japanese) bread crumbs**
- 5 **medium green tomatoes, cut into 1/4-inch slices**

Oil for deep-fat frying

Salt

In three separate shallow bowls, place the flour, eggs and bread crumbs. Dip the tomatoes in flour, then in eggs; coat with bread crumbs.

In an electric skillet or deep-fat fryer, heat oil to 375°. Fry tomatoes, a few at a time, for 2-3 minutes on each side or until golden brown. Drain on paper towels. Sprinkle with salt. Serve immediately.

red rice

PREP: 20 min. | **BAKE:** 45 min. | **YIELD:** 6 servings.

This colorful rice dish features enough bacon flavor to satisfy the deepest craving! Plus, the hot pepper sauce adds a zip to satisfy those with spicier tastes.

MILDRED SHERRER, FORT WORTH, TEXAS

- 5 **bacon strips**
- 1 **medium onion, diced**
- 2 **cups chopped seeded peeled fresh tomatoes**
- 1 **cup uncooked long grain rice**
- 1 **cup tomato juice *or* water**
- 1 **cup finely chopped fully cooked ham**
- 1/2 **teaspoon salt**
- 1/8 **teaspoon pepper**
- 1/8 **teaspoon hot pepper sauce**

In a large skillet, cook bacon until crisp. Remove to paper towels; drain. Discard all but 2 tablespoons of drippings. Saute onion in drippings until tender. Add bacon and remaining ingredients. Cook, covered, over medium-low heat for 10 minutes.

Spoon into a 1-1/2-qt. baking dish. Cover and bake at 350° for 45 minutes or until rice is tender, stirring occasionally.

corn spoon bread

PREP: 15 min. | **COOK:** 3 hours | **YIELD:** 8 servings.

I prepare this comforting side dish with all of my holiday meals. It's moister than corn pudding made in the oven, plus the cream cheese is a nice addition. It goes great with Thanksgiving turkey or Christmas ham. TAMARA ELLEFSON, FREDERIC, WISCONSIN

1	package (8 ounces) cream cheese, softened
1/3	cup sugar
1	cup 2% milk
1/2	cup egg substitute
2	tablespoons butter, melted
1	teaspoon salt
1/4	teaspoon ground nutmeg

Dash pepper

2-1/3	cups frozen corn, thawed
1	can (14-3/4 ounces) cream-style corn
1	package (8-1/2 ounces) corn bread/muffin mix

In a large bowl, beat the cream cheese and sugar until smooth. Gradually beat in milk. Beat in the egg substitute, butter, salt, nutmeg and pepper until blended. Stir in the corn and cream-style corn. Stir in the corn bread mix just until moistened.

Pour into a greased 3-qt. slow cooker. Cover and cook on high for 3-4 hours or until center is almost set.

corn spoon bread

creamy succotash

creamy succotash

PREP: 10 min. | **COOK:** 20 min. + cooling | **YIELD:** 10 servings.

This succotash is my sister Jenny's creation. When I saw her make it, I didn't think the combination would be very tasty. But after one bite, I quickly changed my mind and have been fixing it ever since! SHANNON KOENE, BLACKSBURG, VIRGINIA

4	cups frozen lima beans
1	cup water
4	cups frozen corn
2/3	cup reduced-fat mayonnaise
2	teaspoons Dijon mustard
1/2	teaspoon onion powder
1/2	teaspoon garlic powder
1/4	teaspoon salt
1/4	teaspoon pepper
2	medium tomatoes, finely chopped
1	small onion, finely chopped

In a large saucepan, bring lima beans and water to a boil. Reduce heat; cover and simmer for 10 minutes. Add corn; return to a boil. Reduce heat; cover and simmer 5-6 minutes longer or until the vegetables are tender. Drain; cool for 10-15 minutes.

Meanwhile, in a large bowl, combine the mayonnaise, mustard, onion powder, garlic powder, salt and pepper. Stir in the bean mixture, tomatoes and onion. Serve immediately or refrigerate until ready to serve.

dirty rice

PREP/TOTAL TIME: 30 min. | **YIELD:** 10-12 servings.

This is an old Louisiana recipe that I've had longer than I can remember. It's a very popular Southern dish. To turn this into a main meal, simply add more sausage and chicken livers.

LUM DAY, BASTROP, LOUISIANA

- 1/2 pound bulk pork sausage
- 1/2 pound chicken livers, chopped
- 1 cup chopped onion
- 1/2 cup chopped celery
- 1/3 cup sliced green onions
- 2 tablespoons minced fresh parsley
- 3 tablespoons butter
- 1 garlic clove, minced
- 1 can (10-1/2 ounces) chicken broth
- 1/2 teaspoon dried basil
- 1/2 teaspoon dried thyme
- 1/2 teaspoon salt
- 1/4 teaspoon pepper
- 1/4 teaspoon hot pepper sauce
- 3 cups cooked rice

In a large skillet, cook sausage for 2-3 minutes; stir in chicken livers. Cook 5-7 minutes more or until sausage and chicken livers are no longer pink; drain and set aside.

In the same skillet, saute the onion, celery, green onions and parsley in butter until the vegetables are tender. Add garlic; cook 1 minute longer. Add broth, basil, thyme, salt, pepper and hot pepper sauce. Stir in rice, sausage and chicken livers. Heat through, stirring constantly.

fried pickle coins

PREP: 20 min. | **COOK:** 5 min./batch | **YIELD:** 16 servings.

These puffy golden bites make a delicious accompaniment to a burger or a sandwich. Or serve them with ranch dressing for a fun appetizer.

AMANDA THORNTON, ALEXANDRIA, KENTUCKY

- 2 cups all-purpose flour
- 1 teaspoon garlic powder
- 1 teaspoon ground mustard
- 1 teaspoon dill weed
- 1 teaspoon paprika
- 1/2 teaspoon garlic salt
- 1/2 teaspoon cayenne pepper
- 1/4 teaspoon pepper
- 2 eggs
- 3 tablespoons 2% milk
- 1 garlic clove, minced
- 3 cups dill pickle slices

Oil for deep-fat frying

Ranch salad dressing and prepared mustard, optional

In a shallow bowl, combine the first eight ingredients. In another shallow bowl, whisk the eggs, milk and garlic. Drain pickles and pat dry. Coat pickles with flour mixture, then dip in egg mixture; coat again with flour mixture.

In an electric skillet or deep-fat fryer, heat oil to 375°. Fry pickles, about 10 at a time, for 1-2 minutes or until golden brown, turning once. Drain on paper towels. Serve warm with ranch dressing and mustard if desired.

vidalia onion bake

PREP: 25 min. | **BAKE:** 20 min. | **YIELD:** 8 servings.

The mild taste of Vidalias makes this bake appealing to onion lovers and nonfans alike. It's an excellent accompaniment to beef, pork or chicken.

KATRINA STITT, ZEPHYRHILLS, FLORIDA

- 6 large sweet onions, sliced (about 12 cups)
- 1/2 cup butter, cubed
- 2 cups crushed butter-flavored crackers
- 1 cup shredded Parmesan cheese
- 1/2 cup shredded cheddar cheese
- 1/4 cup shredded Romano cheese

In a large skillet, saute onions in butter until tender and liquid has evaporated. Place half of the onions in a greased 2-qt. baking dish; sprinkle with half of the cracker crumbs and cheeses. Repeat layers.

Bake, uncovered, at 325° for 20-25 minutes or until golden brown.

vidalia onion bake

bacon collard greens

PREP: 25 min. | **COOK:** 55 min. | **YIELD:** 9 servings.

Collard greens are a staple vegetable of Southern cuisine. This nutrient-packed side dish is often made with smoked or salt-cured meats such as ham hocks, pork or fatback. MARSHA ANKENEY, NICEVILLE, FLORIDA

2	**pounds collard greens**
4	**thick-sliced bacon strips, chopped**
1	**cup chopped sweet onion**
5	**cups reduced-sodium chicken broth**
1	**cup sun-dried tomatoes (not packed in oil), chopped**
1/2	**teaspoon garlic powder**
1/4	**teaspoon salt**
1/4	**teaspoon crushed red pepper flakes**

Trim thick stems from collard greens; coarsely chop leaves. In a Dutch oven, saute bacon for 3 minutes. Add onion; cook 8-9 minutes longer or until onion is tender and bacon is crisp. Add greens; cook just until wilted.

Stir in the remaining ingredients. Bring to a boil. Reduce heat; cover and simmer for 45-50 minutes or until greens are tender.

pot likker

Pot likker, also known as pot or collard liquor, is the greenish, meat-flavored liquid that results from slow-cooking collard greens. Pot likker is used as a base for soups and stews, poured over rice or grits with hot sauce, or soaked up directly on the plate with corn bread or rolls.

pickled green tomato relish

PREP: 1 hour + standing | **PROCESS:** 15 min./batch | **YIELD:** 8 pints.

I reach for this recipe when I'm left with green tomatoes at the end of summer. Friends and family are so happy to receive the sweet-sour relish that they often return the empty jar and ask for a refill!

MARY GILL, FLORENCE, OREGON

7	pounds green tomatoes (about 20 medium)
4	large onions
2	large red onions
3	large green peppers
2	large sweet red peppers
4	teaspoons canning salt
5	cups cider vinegar
4	cups sugar
2	tablespoons celery seed
4	teaspoons mustard seed

Cut the tomatoes, onions and peppers into wedges. In a food processor, cover and process vegetables in batches until finely chopped. Stir in salt. Divide mixture between two strainers and place each over a bowl. Let stand for 3 hours.

Discard liquid from bowls. Place vegetables in a stockpot; stir in the vinegar, sugar, celery seed and mustard seed. Bring to a boil. Reduce heat; simmer, uncovered, for 30-35 minutes or until thickened.

Carefully ladle hot mixture into hot pint jars, leaving 1/2-in. headspace. Remove air bubbles; wipe rims and adjust lids. Process for 15 minutes in a boiling-water canner.

EDITOR'S NOTE: The processing time listed is for altitudes of 1,000 feet or less. For altitudes up to 3,000 feet, add 5 minutes; 6,000 feet, add 10 minutes; 8,000 feet, add 15 minutes; 10,000 feet, add 20 minutes.

southern fried okra

PREP/TOTAL TIME: 30 min. | **YIELD:** 2 servings.

Nothing beats a batch of okra straight from the garden. Golden brown, with a little fresh green color showing through, these okra nuggets are crunchy and flavorful. My sons like to dip the them in ketchup.

PAM DUNCAN, SUMMERS, ARKANSAS

1-1/2	cups sliced fresh *or* frozen okra, thawed
3	tablespoons buttermilk
2	tablespoons all-purpose flour
2	tablespoons cornmeal
1/4	teaspoon salt
1/4	teaspoon garlic herb seasoning blend
1/8	teaspoon pepper

Oil for deep-fat frying

Additional salt and pepper, optional

Pat okra dry with paper towels. Place buttermilk in a shallow bowl. In another shallow bowl, combine the flour, cornmeal, salt, seasoning blend and pepper. Dip okra in buttermilk, then roll in cornmeal mixture.

In an electric skillet or deep-fat fryer, heat 1 in. of oil to 375°. Fry okra, a few pieces at a time, for 1-1/2 to 2-1/2 minutes on each side or until golden brown. Drain on paper towels. Season with additional salt and pepper if desired.

grilled corn on the cob

PREP: 20 min. + soaking | **GRILL:** 25 min. | **YIELD:** 8 servings.

I had never tasted grilled corn until my sister-in-law served it for supper one summer. What a treat! So simple yet delicious, grilled corn is now a must for any of my summer menus.

ANGELA LEINENBACH, MECHANICSVLLE, VIRGINIA

8	medium ears sweet corn
1/2	cup butter, softened
2	tablespoons minced fresh basil
2	tablespoons minced fresh parsley
1/2	teaspoon salt

Soak corn in cold water for 20 minutes. Meanwhile, in a small bowl, combine the butter, basil, parsley and salt. Carefully peel back corn husks to within 1 in. of bottoms; remove silk. Spread butter mixture over corn.

Rewrap corn in husks and secure with kitchen string. Grill corn, covered, over medium heat for 25-30 minutes or until tender, turning occasionally. Cut the strings and peel back the husks.

grilled corn on the cob

old-fashioned macaroni and cheese

PREP: 15 min. | **BAKE:** 45 min. | **YIELD:** 12-16 servings.

Bring back the taste of days gone by with this ooey-gooey mac-and-cheese classic. A bit of ground mustard and hot pepper sauce give it a little kick.
JAMES BACKMAN, CENTRALIA, WASHINGTON

3-1/2	cups uncooked elbow macaroni (about 12 ounces)
1/4	cup butter, cubed
1/4	cup all-purpose flour
1	teaspoon salt
3/4	teaspoon ground mustard
1/2	teaspoon pepper
	Few dashes hot pepper sauce
3-1/2	cups milk
5	cups (20 ounces) shredded cheddar cheese, *divided*

Cook macaroni in boiling water until almost tender; drain. Meanwhile, in a Dutch oven, melt butter. Stir in the flour, salt, mustard, pepper and pepper sauce until smooth. Cook for 1 minute or until bubbly. Stir in the macaroni, milk and 4 cups cheese.

Transfer to an ungreased 13-in. x 9-in. baking dish. Cover and bake at 350° for 45-50 minutes or until bubbly. Uncover; sprinkle with the remaining cheese. Let stand for 5 minutes before serving..

old-fashioned macaroni and cheese

hoppin' john

hoppin' john

PREP/TOTAL TIME: 15 min. | **YIELD:** 2 servings.

A New Year's tradition, this mildly flavored rice dish is a great accompaniment to almost any meat entree.
BETH WALL, INMAN, SOUTH CAROLINA

1/4	cup chopped sweet red pepper
1/4	cup chopped green pepper
2	tablespoons chopped onion
1/4	teaspoon garlic powder
1/8	teaspoon salt
1	tablespoon butter
2/3	cup canned black-eyed peas, rinsed and drained
2/3	cup cooked rice

In a small skillet, saute the peppers, onion, garlic powder and salt in butter for 4-5 minutes or until vegetables are tender. Stir in the peas and rice; heat through, stirring occasionally.

corn bread dressing with oysters

PREP: 10 min. | **BAKE:** 45 min. | **YIELD:** 12-15 servings.

This dressing, baked separately from the turkey, is simply delicious. The secret is to prepare the corn bread first, let it cool and then crumble it to form the base for the rest of the ingredients. My father always added oysters to give the dressing a special flavor.
NELL BASS, MACON, GEORGIA

8	to 10 cups coarsely crumbled corn bread
2	slices white bread, toasted and torn into small pieces

2 hard-cooked eggs, chopped
2 cups chopped celery
1 cup chopped onion
1 pint shucked oysters, drained and chopped *or* 2 cans (8 ounces *each*) whole oysters, drained and chopped
1/2 cup egg substitute
1 teaspoon poultry seasoning
5 to 6 cups turkey *or* chicken broth

Combine the first eight ingredients in a large bowl. Stir in enough broth until the mixture is very wet. Pour into a greased 13-in. x 9-in. baking dish or shallow 3-qt. baking dish.

Bake, uncovered, at 400° for 45 minutes or until it is lightly browned.

fried cabbage

PREP/TOTAL TIME: 20 min. | **YIELD:** 6 servings.

Fried cabbage is tasty with potatoes, deviled eggs and corn bread. When I was young, my family grew our own cabbage and potatoes. It was fun to put our crop to good use in the kitchen.
BERNICE MORRIS, MARSHFIELD, MISSOURI

2 tablespoons butter
1 teaspoon sugar
1/2 teaspoon salt
1/4 teaspoon crushed red pepper flakes

fried cabbage

1/8 teaspoon pepper
6 cups coarsely chopped cabbage
1 tablespoon water

In a large skillet, melt butter over medium heat. Stir in the sugar, salt, pepper flakes and pepper. Add the cabbage and water. Cook for 5-6 minutes or until tender, stirring occasionally.

herb-crusted sweet onion rings

PREP/TOTAL TIME: 30 min. | **YIELD:** 8 servings.

These are the ultimate onion rings! Lightly battered and seasoned with herbs and Dijon mustard, these cook up crisp and golden brown.
DENISE PATTERSON, BAINBRIDGE, OHIO

1 cup all-purpose flour
1 cup beer *or* nonalcoholic beer
2 tablespoons Dijon mustard
2 teaspoons salt-free Italian herb seasoning
1 teaspoon salt
1/4 teaspoon cayenne pepper
2 large sweet onions

Oil for deep-fat frying

In a shallow bowl, whisk the first six ingredients. Cut onions into 1/4-in. slices and separate into rings. Dip in flour mixture.

In an electric skillet or deep-fat fryer, heat 1 in. of oil to 375°. Fry onion rings, a few at a time, for 1-2 minutes on each side or until golden brown. Drain on paper towels. Serve immediately.

sweet potato bake

PREP: 35 min. | **BAKE:** 20 min. + standing | **YIELD:** 10-12 servings.

This is an easy dish to prepare and is a perfect addition to that special holiday meal. The topping is flavorful and gives a nice contrast of textures.
PAM HOLLOWAY, MARION, LOUISIANA

7	large sweet potatoes (about 6 pounds), peeled and cubed
1/4	cup butter, cubed
1/2	cup orange marmalade
1/4	cup orange juice
1/4	cup packed brown sugar
2	teaspoons salt
1	teaspoon ground ginger

TOPPING:

12	oatmeal cookies, crumbled
6	tablespoons butter, softened

Place sweet potatoes in a Dutch oven and cover with water. Bring to a boil. Reduce heat; cover and cook just for 10-15 minutes or until tender. Drain

Mash potatoes with butter. Add the marmalade, orange juice, brown sugar, salt and ginger. Transfer to a greased 13-in. x 9-in. baking dish. Toss cookie crumbs with butter; sprinkle over the top.

Bake, uncovered, at 400° for 20 minutes or until browned. Let stand for 15 minutes before serving.

sweet potato bake

amaretto-peach preserves

amaretto-peach preserves

PREP: 1-1/4 hours | **PROCESS:** 10 min. | **YIELD:** 5 half-pints.

Chock-full of peaches, raisins and pecans, this lovely conserve enhances ordinary slices of toast.
REDAWNA KALYNCHUK, SEXSMITH, ALBERTA

1	cup golden raisins
3/4	cup boiling water
2	pounds peaches, peeled and chopped
4	teaspoons grated orange peel
1/3	cup orange juice
2	tablespoons lemon juice
3	cups sugar
1/2	cup chopped pecans
3	tablespoons Amaretto

Place raisins in a small bowl. Cover with boiling water; let stand for 5 minutes. Place raisins with liquid in a large saucepan. Add peaches and orange peel. Bring to a boil. Reduce heat; cover and simmer for 10-15 minutes or until peaches are tender.

Stir in orange and lemon juices; return to a boil. Add sugar. Cook, uncovered, over medium heat for 25-30 minutes or until thickened, stirring occasionally. Add pecans; cook 5 minutes longer. Remove from the heat; stir in Amaretto.

Carefully ladle hot mixture into hot sterilized half-pint jars, leaving 1/4-in. headspace. Remove air bubbles; wipe rims and adjust lids. Process in a boiling-water canner for 5 minutes.

EDITOR'S NOTE: The processing time listed is for altitudes of 1,000 feet or less. Add 1 minute to the processing time for each 1,000 feet of additional altitude.

loaded red potato casserole

PREP: 25 min. | **BAKE:** 20 min. | **YIELD:** 9 servings.

This potato casserole has the same flavor of the potato skins you can order as a restaurant appetizer. It's an ideal dish for tailgating and potlucks.

CHARLANE GATHY, LEXINGTON, KENTUCKY

16	small red potatoes
1/2	cup 2% milk
1/4	cup butter, cubed
1/2	teaspoon pepper
1/8	teaspoon salt
1-1/2	cups (6 ounces) shredded cheddar cheese, *divided*
1/2	cup crumbled cooked bacon
1	cup (8 ounces) sour cream
2	tablespoons minced chives

Place potatoes in a Dutch oven and cover with water. Bring to a boil. Reduce heat; cover and cook for 15-20 minutes or until tender. Drain.

Mash potatoes with the milk, butter, pepper and salt. Transfer to a greased 13-in. x 9-in. baking dish. Sprinkle with 1 cup cheese and bacon.

Dollop with sour cream; sprinkle with chives and remaining cheese. Bake, uncovered, at 350° for 20-25 minutes or until cheese is melted.

easy mincing and chopping

To mince or chop, hold the handle of a chef's knife with one hand, and rest the fingers of your other hand on the top of the blade near the tip. Using the handle to guide and apply pressure, move the knife in an arc across the food with a rocking motion until the pieces of food are the desired size. Mincing results in pieces no larger than 1/8 in., and chopping can produce 1/4-in. to 1/2-in. pieces.

LOW COUNTRY BOIL

main entrees

low country boil

PREP: 20 min. | **COOK:** 40 min. | **YIELD:** 4 servings.

This picnic-style medley of shrimp, crab, sausage, corn and spuds is a specialty of South Carolina cuisine. It is also commonly dubbed Beaufort Stew or Frogmore Stew, in recognition of both of the Low Country communities that lay claim to its origin. No matter what you call it, I guarantee this one-pot wonder won't disappoint!

MAGESWARI ELAGUPILLAI, VICTORVILLE, CALIFORNIA

2	quarts water
1	bottle (12 ounces) beer
2	tablespoons seafood seasoning
1-1/2	teaspoons salt
4	medium red potatoes, cut into wedges
1	medium sweet onion, cut into wedges
4	medium ears sweet corn, cut in half
1/3	pound smoked chorizo *or* kielbasa, cut into 1-inch slices
3	tablespoons olive oil
6	large garlic cloves, minced
1	tablespoon ground cumin
1	tablespoon minced fresh cilantro
1/2	teaspoon paprika
1/2	teaspoon pepper
1	pound uncooked large shrimp, deveined
1	pound uncooked snow crab legs

Optional condiments: seafood cocktail sauce, lemon wedges and melted butter

In a stockpot, combine the water, beer, seafood seasoning and salt; add potatoes and onion. Bring to a boil. Reduce heat; simmer, uncovered, for 10 minutes. Add corn and chorizo; simmer 10-12 minutes longer or until potatoes and corn are tender.

Meanwhile, in a small skillet, heat oil. Add the garlic, cumin, cilantro, paprika and pepper. Cook and stir over medium heat for 1 minute.

Stir the shrimp, crab legs and garlic mixture into the stockpot; cook for 4-6 minutes or until shrimp and crab turn pink. Drain; transfer seafood mixture to a large serving bowl. Serve with condiments of your choice.

low country boil

Similar to crawfish boils in Louisiana, the famous Low Country boils of South Carolina are more of an event than a dish! Popular fare for picnics, family reunions, trips to the beach and even camping, this one-pot meal is best served on a large platter on a newspaper-covered table and eaten with the fingers.

chipotle pork tenderloins

PREP: 20 min. + marinating | **GRILL:** 25 min.
YIELD: 9 servings (5 cups salsa).

This pork tenderloin beats all others! The recipe came from a family member and is such a treat. Fresh strawberries and avocado in the salsa help cool the spicy heat of the pork.

PRISCILLA GILBERT, INDIAN HARBOUR BEACH, FLORIDA

1	cup sliced onion
1/2	cup chipotle peppers in adobo sauce, chopped
1/4	cup lime juice
1-1/2	teaspoons minced garlic
3	pork tenderloins (1 pound *each*)

STRAWBERRY SALSA:

5	cups sliced fresh strawberries
1/4	cup thinly sliced green onions
1/4	cup minced fresh cilantro
1/4	cup lime juice
1/4	teaspoon salt
1	medium ripe avocado, peeled and chopped

In a large resealable plastic bag, combine the onion, chipotle peppers, lime juice and garlic; add pork. Seal bag and turn to coat; refrigerate for at least 1 hour.

Prepare grill for indirect heat. Drain and discard marinade. Grill pork, covered, over indirect medium heat for 25-40 minutes or until a meat thermometer reads 160°. Let stand for 5 minutes before slicing.

For salsa, in a large bowl, combine the strawberries, green onions, cilantro, lime juice and salt. Gently stir in avocado. Serve with pork.

ROASTED CHIPOTLE PORK TENDERLOINS: Drain and discard marinade from pork. Place tenderloins on a rack in a shallow roasting pan. Bake, uncovered, at 425° for 25-30 minutes or until a meat thermometer reads 160°. Serve as directed.

chipotle pork tenderloins

grilled stuffed pork chops

PREP/TOTAL TIME: 30 min. | **YIELD:** 4 servings.

I live in Texas, where the summers get hot, so I do a lot of my cooking outdoors on the grill. You'll enjoy the one-of-a-kind combination of stuffing and sauce in these zesty chops. DIANNE GATES, CYPRESS, TEXAS

1	cup medium picante sauce
2	tablespoons honey
1	teaspoon Worcestershire sauce
4	pork chops (1 inch thick)
1/2	pound bulk spicy pork sausage
1/2	teaspoon garlic powder
1/4	teaspoon pepper
1/4	cup prepared zesty Italian salad dressing

In a small bowl, combine the picante sauce, honey and Worcestershire sauce; stir until honey is dissolved. Divide the sauce into two small bowls; set aside.

Cut a deep slit in each chop, forming a pocket. Stuff with sausage; secure with toothpicks. Sprinkle chops with garlic powder and pepper. Brush each side with Italian dressing.

Grill, covered, over medium heat for 5 minutes on each side. Grill 10-15 minutes longer or until meat juices run clear, basting twice with sauce from one bowl. Remove toothpicks. Serve with sauce from the second bowl.

pork pockets

When creating pockets in pork chops, use a paring knife to make a slit in the chop's fatty side. Cut almost to the other side but not through the chop. Spoon the stuffing mixture into the pocket and secure the opening with toothpicks.

barbecued beef short ribs

PREP: 25 min. | **COOK:** 5 hours | **YIELD:** 8 servings.

These tender, slow-cooked ribs with a tangy sauce are a cinch to make. They're great for picnics and parties. ERIN GLASS, WHITE HALL, MARYLAND

4	pounds bone-in beef short ribs, trimmed
2	tablespoons canola oil
1	large sweet onion, halved and sliced
1	bottle (12 ounces) chili sauce
3/4	cup plum preserves *or* preserves of your choice
2	tablespoons brown sugar
2	tablespoons red wine vinegar
2	tablespoons Worcestershire sauce
2	tablespoons Dijon mustard
1/4	teaspoon ground cloves

In a large skillet, brown ribs in oil in batches. Place onion in a 5-qt. slow cooker; add ribs. Cover and cook on low for 4 to 5 hours or until meat is tender.

In a small saucepan, combine the remaining ingredients. Cook and stir over medium heat for 4-6 minutes or until heated through.

Remove the ribs from the slow cooker. Skim the fat from cooking juices. Return ribs to slow cooker; pour sauce over ribs. Cover and cook on high for 25-30 minutes or until sauce is thickened.

mustard fried catfish

PREP/TOTAL TIME: 20 min. | **YIELD:** 4 servings.

Here's one of my favorite recipes. The fish turns out so delicious and flaky, and it's easy to prepare, too. I've also used orange roughy and cod with good results. BARBARA KEITH, FAUCETT, MISSOURI

2/3	cup yellow cornmeal
1/3	cup all-purpose flour

1/2	teaspoon salt
1/4	teaspoon paprika
1/4	teaspoon pepper
1/8	teaspoon cayenne pepper
1/2	cup prepared mustard
4	catfish fillets (6 ounces *each*)

Oil for frying

In a shallow bowl, combine the first six ingredients. Spread mustard over both sides of the fillets; coat fillets with the cornmeal mixture.

In an electric skillet or deep-fat fryer, heat oil to 375°. Fry fillets, a few at a time, for 2-3 minutes on each side or until fish flakes easily with a fork. Drain on paper towels.

barbecued sticky ribs

PREP: 10 min. | **BAKE:** 1 hour 20 min. | **YIELD:** 6-8 servings.

There's nothing like a rack of barbecued ribs to satisfy a hearty appetite! These make a great summertime treat, but our family also traditionally enjoys them alongside side dishes of coleslaw and beans at big game-day parties in the fall and winter.
JACKIE REMSBERG, LA CANADA, CALIFORNIA

3/4	teaspoon garlic powder
1	teaspoon salt
1/2	teaspoon pepper
3-1/2 to 4-1/2	pounds pork spareribs (2 racks)

SAUCE:

1	can (10-3/4 ounces) condensed tomato soup, undiluted
1	small onion, chopped
1	cup water
1/2	cup light corn syrup
1/2	cup ketchup
1/4	cup cider vinegar
2	tablespoons Worcestershire sauce
2	teaspoons chili powder
1	teaspoon hot pepper sauce
1/2	teaspoon ground cinnamon

Combine the garlic powder, salt and pepper; rub onto both sides of ribs. Place in a single layer in a 15-in. x 10-in. x 1-in. baking pan.

Bake at 325° for 30-35 minutes; drain. Combine sauce ingredients; pour over ribs. Bake 50-60 minutes longer or until meat is tender, basting occasionally. Cut into serving-size pieces.

cheese-filled meat loaf

PREP: 35 min. | **BAKE:** 65 min. + standing | **YIELD:** 6 servings.

Swirled with a filling of sour cream, cheddar cheese and stuffed olives, my mother's meat loaf is something special. It's a timeless centerpiece for Sunday dinner or any festive occasion.

SUSAN HANSEN, AUBURN, ALABAMA

- 1/2 cup milk
- 2 eggs, lightly beaten
- 1 tablespoon Worcestershire sauce
- 1 cup crushed cornflakes
- 1/2 cup finely chopped onion
- 3 tablespoons finely chopped celery
- 1 teaspoon salt
- 1/2 teaspoon ground mustard
- 1/2 teaspoon rubbed sage
- 1/4 teaspoon pepper
- 1-1/2 pounds ground beef
- 1 cup (8 ounces) sour cream
- 1 cup (4 ounces) finely shredded cheddar cheese
- 1/2 cup sliced pimiento-stuffed olives

In a large bowl, combine the first 10 ingredients. Crumble beef over mixture and mix well. On a large piece of heavy-duty foil, pat beef mixture into a 14-in. x 10-in. rectangle. Spread sour cream to within 1/2 in. of edges. Sprinkle with cheese and olives.

Roll up, jelly-roll style, starting with a short side and peeling away foil while rolling. Seal seam and ends. Place seam side down in a greased 13-in. x 9-in. baking dish.

Bake, uncovered, at 350° for 65-75 minutes or until meat is no longer pink and a meat thermometer reads 160°. Let stand for 10 minutes before slicing.

cheese-filled meat loaf

pierside salmon patties

pierside salmon patties

PREP: 15 min. | **BAKE:** 30 min. | **YIELD:** 6 servings.

A lemony dill sauce enhances the flavor of the salmon in this delightful entree I served my card-player friends at a "Let's Go Fishing" luncheon. I hosted the gathering at our summer lake cottage.

MARTHA CONAWAY, PATASKALA, OHIO

- 2 eggs, lightly beaten
- 1 cup 2% milk
- 2 tablespoons lemon juice
- 3 cups coarsely crushed saltines (about 66 crackers)
- 2 teaspoons finely chopped onion
- 1/4 teaspoon salt
- 1/4 teaspoon pepper
- 2 cans (14-3/4 ounces *each*) salmon, drained, bones and skin removed

DILL SAUCE:

- 2 tablespoons butter
- 2 tablespoons all-purpose flour
- 1 teaspoon snipped fresh dill *or* 1/2 teaspoon dill weed
- 1/4 teaspoon salt

Dash pepper

Dash nutmeg

- 1-1/2 cups milk

In a large bowl, beat the eggs, milk, lemon juice, saltines, onion, salt and pepper. Stir in the salmon. Shape into twelve 3-in. patties.

Place in a greased 15-in. x 10-in. x 1-in. baking pan. Bake at 350° for 30-35 minutes or until lightly browned.

In a small saucepan, melt butter. Stir in the flour, dill, salt, pepper and nutmeg until blended. Gradually add milk. Bring to a boil; cook and stir for 2 minutes or until thickened. Serve with salmon patties.

holiday baked ham

PREP: 20 min. | **BAKE:** 2 hours 50 min. + standing
YIELD: 30 servings.

I've made this special baked ham many times over the years for my children and grandchildren. They are all very fond of it. Honey, brown sugar and pan juices create a succulent glaze.
MARY PADGETT, SAVANNAH, GEORGIA

1	fully cooked bone-in ham (10 to 12 pounds)
2	teaspoons whole cloves, *divided*
1	large onion, chopped
2	garlic cloves, minced
1	teaspoon dried oregano
1	teaspoon dried basil
1/2	teaspoon pepper
1	cup packed brown sugar, *divided*
1/2	cup minced fresh parsley
3	cups ginger ale
1	cup honey
1	can (16 ounces) pineapple slices, drained

Remove skin from ham; score the surface, making diamond shapes 1/2 in. deep. Insert a clove in every other diamond; set remaining cloves aside.

Place ham on a rack in a shallow roasting pan. Combine the onion, garlic, oregano, basil and pepper; pat onto ham. Combine 1/2 cup brown sugar and parsley; sprinkle over top of ham. Pour ginger ale around ham.

Bake, uncovered, at 350° for 2 hours, basting often.

Remove ham from pan; set aside. Drain pan juices, reserving 3 tablespoons. For glaze, combine honey, remaining brown sugar and reserved pan juices in a small bowl.

Increase oven temperature to 400°. Return ham to pan. Insert remaining cloves into ham. Spoon half of the glaze over ham. Bake for 20 minutes.

Place pineapple on ham; drizzle with remaining glaze. Bake 30 minutes longer or until a meat thermometer reads 140°. Let stand for 15 minutes before carving.

breaded italian pork chops

PREP/TOTAL TIME: 25 min. | **YIELD:** 4 servings.

Italian salad dressing and seasoned bread crumbs add a hint of Italian flavor to these nicely coated pork chops. These chops are so quick and simple to prepare, and everyone loves them!
JOAN LOCKWOOD, SAN JOSE, CALIFORNIA

1/2	cup biscuit/baking mix
1/3	cup prepared Italian salad dressing
1/2	cup seasoned bread crumbs

louisiana red beans and rice

4	bone-in pork loin chops (1/2 inch thick and 7 ounces *each*)
2	tablespoons canola oil

Place the biscuit mix, salad dressing and bread crumbs in separate shallow bowls. Coat pork chops in biscuit mix, then dip in dressing and coat with crumbs.

In a large skillet, brown pork chops in oil over medium-high heat for 2-3 minutes on each side. Reduce heat; cook, uncovered, for 10-15 minutes or until juices run clear.

louisiana red beans and rice

PREP: 20 min. | **COOK:** 8 hours | **YIELD:** 9 servings.

Smoked turkey sausage and red pepper flakes add zip to this saucy, slow-cooked version of the New Orleans classic. For extra heat, add red pepper sauce at the table. JULIA BUSHREE, GEORGETOWN, TEXAS

4	cans (16 ounces *each*) kidney beans, rinsed and drained
1	can (14-1/2 ounces) diced tomatoes, undrained
1	package (14 ounces) smoked turkey sausage, sliced
1	cup chicken broth
3	celery ribs, chopped
1	large onion, chopped
1	medium green pepper, chopped
1	small sweet red pepper, chopped
6	garlic cloves, minced
1	bay leaf
1/2	teaspoon crushed red pepper flakes
2	green onions, chopped

Hot cooked rice

In a 4-qt. slow cooker, combine the first 11 ingredients. Cover and cook on low for 8-10 hours or until heated through. Stir before serving. Discard bay leaf.

Sprinkle each serving with onions. Serve with rice.

seafood casserole

PREP: 20 min. | **BAKE:** 40 min. | **YIELD:** 6 servings.

A family favorite, this rice casserole is stuffed with plenty of seafood and veggies. It's hearty, homey and easy to make. NANCY BILLUPS, PRINCETON, IOWA

1	package (6 ounces) long grain and wild rice
1	pound frozen crabmeat, thawed *or* 2-1/2 cups canned lump crabmeat, drained
1	pound cooked medium shrimp, peeled, deveined and cut into 1/2-inch pieces
2	celery ribs, chopped
1	medium onion, finely chopped
1/2	cup finely chopped green pepper
1	can (4 ounces) mushroom stems and pieces, drained
1	jar (2 ounces) diced pimientos, drained
1	cup mayonnaise
1	cup milk
1/2	teaspoon pepper
Dash	Worcestershire sauce
1/4	cup dry bread crumbs

Cook rice according to package directions. Meanwhile, in a large bowl, combine the crab, shrimp, celery, onion, green pepper, mushrooms and pimientos.

In a small bowl, whisk the mayonnaise, milk, pepper and Worcestershire sauce; stir into the seafood mixture. Stir in the rice.

Transfer to a greased 13-in. x 9-in. baking dish. Sprinkle with bread crumbs. Bake, uncovered, at 375° for 40-50 minutes or until bubbly.

southern pan-fried quail with cream cheese grits

PREP: 40 min. + marinating | **COOK:** 25 min.
YIELD: 8 servings (with 1/2 cup grits and 1/3 cup gravy).

I was introduced to quail (a midsized bird in the pheasant family) when I moved to South Carolina. Now it's one of my favorite entrees.
ATHENA RUSSELL, FLORENCE, SOUTH CAROLINA

1-1/2	cups buttermilk
1-1/2	teaspoons salt, *divided*
1	teaspoon pepper, *divided*
8	split and flattened quail (4 ounces *each*), thawed
1	cup all-purpose flour
1/2	teaspoon onion powder
1/2	teaspoon garlic powder
1/4	teaspoon cayenne pepper

2/3	cup canola oil

GRAVY:

3	tablespoons all-purpose flour
1-1/2	cups heavy whipping cream
1	cup chicken broth
1/4	teaspoon salt
1/4	teaspoon pepper

GRITS:

1	cup uncooked old-fashioned grits
1/2	cup cream cheese, softened
1/2	cup heavy whipping cream
1/4	teaspoon salt
1/4	teaspoon pepper

In a large resealable plastic bag, combine the buttermilk and 1/2 teaspoon each of salt and pepper. Add the quail; seal bag and turn to coat. Refrigerate for 1 hour. Drain and discard marinade.

In a shallow bowl, combine the flour, onion powder, garlic powder, cayenne and remaining salt and pepper. Coat quail with flour mixture.

In a large skillet, cook quail in oil in batches over medium heat for 4-6 minutes on each side or until a meat thermometer reads 165°. Drain on paper towels. Remove to a serving platter and keep warm.

For gravy, stir flour into pan drippings until blended; cook and stir for 4 minutes or until golden brown. Gradually add the cream, broth, salt and pepper. Bring to a boil; cook and stir for 2 minutes or until thickened.

Meanwhile, prepare grits according to package directions. Add the cream cheese, cream, salt and pepper. Cook and stir until cream cheese is melted and grits are heated through. Serve with quail and gravy.

seasoned pork rib roast

PREP: 10 min. + chilling | **BAKE:** 1-1/2 hours + standing
YIELD: 8 servings.

My husband created this recipe and is proud to call it his "house specialty." The simple seasoning also works well on a variety of other meats, including pork chops, beef roast and chicken.

JOYCE KRAMER, DONALSONVILLE, GEORGIA

1	tablespoon garlic powder
1	tablespoon onion powder
1	tablespoon dried marjoram
1	tablespoon dried parsley flakes
1	to 2 teaspoons cayenne pepper
1	bone-in pork rib roast (about 4 pounds)

Combine the garlic powder, onion powder, marjoram, parsley and cayenne; rub over roast. Place in a large shallow glass dish. Cover and refrigerate overnight.

Place roast bone side down in a shallow roasting pan. Bake, uncovered, at 350° 1-1/2 to 1-3/4 hours or until a meat thermometer reads 160°. Let roast stand for 10 minutes before carving.

black bean tamale pie

PREP: 20 min. | **BAKE:** 20 min. | **YIELD:** 6-8 servings.

A packaged corn bread mix speeds the preparation of this Southwestern entree with beef and black beans. My husband really likes it, and guests enjoy this unique Mexican dish as well.

LAURA MORRIS, ST. JOSEPH, MISSOURI

1/2	pound ground beef
1/2	cup chopped onion
1/2	cup chopped green pepper
1	can (15 ounces) black beans, rinsed and drained
1	cup salsa
1	package (8-1/2 ounces) corn bread/muffin mix
1/4	cup milk
1	egg
2	cups (8 ounces) shredded cheddar cheese, *divided*

Sour cream and sliced ripe olives, optional

In a large skillet, cook the beef, onion and green pepper over medium heat until meat is no longer pink; drain. Stir in beans and salsa; set aside. In a large bowl, combine the muffin mix, milk, egg and 1 cup cheese. Pour into a greased 9-in. pie plate. Bake at 375° for 5-6 minutes.

Spoon beef mixture over crust, leaving a 1/2-in. edge. Bake for 15-18 minutes or until crust is golden brown. Sprinkle with remaining cheese. Bake 1-2 minutes longer or until cheese is melted. Serve with sour cream and olives if desired.

black bean tamale pie

blackened chicken

PREP/TOTAL TIME: 25 min. | **YIELD:** 4 servings.

This spicy standout packs a one-two punch of flavor. The grilled chicken is basted with a peppery white sauce. Plus, there's plenty of extra sauce left over for dipping. STEPHANIE KENNEY, FALKVILLE, ALABAMA

1	tablespoon paprika
4	teaspoons sugar, *divided*
1-1/2	teaspoons salt, *divided*
1	teaspoon garlic powder
1	teaspoon dried thyme
1	teaspoon lemon-pepper seasoning
1	teaspoon cayenne pepper
1-1/2	to 2 teaspoons pepper, *divided*
4	boneless skinless chicken breast halves (4 ounces *each*)
1-1/3	cups mayonnaise
2	tablespoons water
2	tablespoons cider vinegar

In a small bowl, combine the paprika, 1 teaspoon sugar, 1 teaspoon salt, garlic powder, thyme, lemon-pepper, cayenne and 1/2 to 1 teaspoon pepper; sprinkle over both sides of chicken. Set aside.

In another bowl, combine the mayonnaise, water, vinegar and remaining sugar, salt and pepper; cover and refrigerate 1 cup for serving. Save remaining sauce for basting.

Grill chicken, covered, over indirect medium heat for 4-6 minutes on each side or until a thermometer reads 170°, basting frequently with the remaining sauce. Serve with reserved sauce.

blackened chicken

porcini ham risotto

porcini ham risotto

PREP/TOTAL TIME: 30 min. | **YIELD:** 8 servings.

The South yields a high rice crop, so risotto, although Italian in origin, is a popular ingredient in many Southern dishes. TASTE OF HOME TEST KITCHEN

1	package (1 ounce) dried porcini mushrooms
2	cups boiling water
1/2	cup chopped shallots
1/3	cup butter, cubed
1	teaspoon minced garlic
1-1/2	cups uncooked arborio rice
1	cup white wine
3	cans (14-1/2 ounces *each*) chicken broth, warmed
1-1/2	cups diced fully cooked ham
5	ounces fontinella cheese, shredded
1/2	teaspoon salt
1/8	teaspoon white pepper

In a large bowl, soak the mushrooms in boiling water for 5 minutes or until completely hydrated; drain. In a Dutch oven, saute mushrooms and shallots in butter for 3-4 minutes or until tender. Add garlic; cook 1 minute longer.

Stir in rice until completely coated with butter. Add wine; cook and stir for 2 minutes or until wine is absorbed. Add one can of broth; cook and stir until broth is absorbed. Repeat with remaining broth, adding one can at a time. Stir in the ham, cheese, salt and pepper; cook until cheese is melted and mixture is heated through.

out of shallots?

Shallots are part of the onion family and have a mild onion-garlic flavor. Onions make an easy substitute if you don't have any shallots on hand. In place of 3 to 4 shallots, use 1 medium onion plus a pinch of garlic powder.

texas-style beef brisket

PREP: 25 min. + marinating | **COOK:** 6-1/2 hours
YIELD: 12 servings.

A friend raved about this recipe, so I thought I would give it a whirl. When my husband told me how much he liked it, I knew it was a keeper!
VIVIAN WARNER, ELKHART, KANSAS

- 3 tablespoons Worcestershire sauce
- 1 tablespoon chili powder
- 2 bay leaves
- 2 garlic cloves, minced
- 1 teaspoon celery salt
- 1 teaspoon pepper
- 1 teaspoon Liquid Smoke, optional
- 1 fresh beef brisket (6 pounds)
- 1/2 cup beef broth

BARBECUE SAUCE:

- 1 medium onion, chopped
- 2 tablespoons canola oil
- 2 garlic cloves, minced
- 1 cup ketchup
- 1/2 cup molasses
- 1/4 cup cider vinegar
- 2 teaspoons chili powder
- 1/2 teaspoon ground mustard

In a large resealable plastic bag, combine the Worcestershire sauce, chili powder, bay leaves, garlic, celery salt, pepper and Liquid Smoke if desired. Cut brisket in half; add to bag. Seal bag and turn to coat. Refrigerate overnight.

Transfer beef to a 5- or 6-qt. slow cooker; add broth. Cover and cook on low for 6-8 hours or until tender.

For sauce, in a small saucepan, saute onion in oil until tender. Add garlic; cook 1 minute longer. Stir in the remaining ingredients; heat through.

Remove brisket from the slow cooker; discard bay leaves. Place 1 cup cooking juices in a measuring cup; skim fat. Add to the barbecue sauce. Discard remaining juices.

Return brisket to the slow cooker; top with sauce mixture. Cover and cook on high for 30 minutes to allow flavors to blend. Thinly slice across the grain; serve with sauce.

crab macaroni & cheese

crab macaroni & cheese

PREP: 45 min. | **BAKE:** 15 min. | **YIELD:** 10 servings.

Crab and mushrooms put a delicious Southern spin on classic macaroni and cheese. It's an upscale casserole perfect for special occasions...but my family could eat it every day!

ANGELA OCHOA, LAKE ELSINORE, CALIFORNIA

1	package (16 ounces) elbow macaroni
6	baby portobello mushrooms
2	green onions, sliced
1	tablespoon plus 1/4 cup butter, *divided*
1/4	cup all-purpose flour
1	teaspoon ground mustard
1	teaspoon pepper
1/2	teaspoon salt
1/4	teaspoon paprika
2-1/2	cups half-and-half cream
1-1/2	cups (6 ounces) shredded part-skim mozzarella cheese, *divided*
1-1/2	cups (6 ounces) shredded medium cheddar cheese, *divided*

TOPPING:

1/2	cup panko (Japanese) bread crumbs
3	tablespoons butter, melted
1	tablespoon dried basil
1-1/2	pounds cooked snow crab legs, meat removed
4	thin slices Swiss cheese
1/4	cup grated Parmesan cheese

Cook macaroni according to package directions. Drain pasta and rinse in cold water.

Meanwhile, in a large skillet, saute mushrooms and onions in 1 tablespoon butter until tender; set aside.

In a large saucepan, melt the remaining butter. Stir in the flour, mustard, pepper, salt and paprika until smooth; gradually add cream. Bring to a boil; cook and stir for 2 minutes or until thickened. Stir in 3/4 cup each mozzarella and cheddar cheeses until blended. Remove from the heat; fold in the macaroni.

In a small bowl, combine the bread crumbs, butter and basil. Transfer half of the macaroni mixture into a greased 13-in. x 9-in. baking dish. Layer with reserved mushroom mixture, remaining macaroni mixture, mozzarella and cheddar cheeses. Top with crab and Swiss cheese. Sprinkle with crumb mixture and Parmesan cheese.

Bake at 350° for 15-20 minutes or until golden brown. Let stand for 5 minutes before serving.

southern fried chicken

PREP: 25 min. | **COOK:** 45 min. | **YIELD:** 6 servings.

This is a Southern classic! It's not authentic without well-seasoned Creamy Gravy.

TASTE OF HOME TEST KITCHEN

1	cup all-purpose flour
1	teaspoon onion powder
1	teaspoon paprika
3/4	teaspoon salt
1/2	teaspoon rubbed sage
1/2	teaspoon pepper
1/4	teaspoon dried thyme
1	egg
1/2	cup milk
1	broiler/fryer chicken (3 to 3-1/2 pounds), cut up

Oil for frying

CREAMY GRAVY:

1/3	cup all-purpose flour
1/4	teaspoon salt
1/4	teaspoon dried thyme
1/4	to 1/2 teaspoon pepper
2-1/2	cups milk
1/2	cup heavy whipping cream

In a large resealable plastic bag, combine the first seven ingredients. In a shallow bowl, beat egg and milk. Dip chicken pieces into egg mixture, then add to flour mixture, a few pieces at a time, and shake to coat.

In a skillet, heat 1/4 in. of oil; fry chicken until browned. Cover and simmer for 35-40 minutes or until juices run clear and chicken is tender, turning occasionally. Uncover and cook 5 minutes longer. Drain on paper towels and keep warm.

Drain skillet, reserving 3 tablespoons drippings. For gravy, in a small bowl, combine the flour, salt, thyme and pepper. Gradually whisk in milk and cream until smooth; add to skillet. Bring to a boil over medium heat; cook and stir for 2 minutes or until thickened. Serve with chicken.

old-fashioned chicken pot pie

In a large bowl, combine the flour, baking powder, sugar, salt and cream of tartar. Cut in butter until mixture resembles coarse crumbs; stir in milk just until moistened. Turn onto a lightly floured surface; knead 8-10 times. Pat or roll out to 1/2-in. thickness. Cut with a floured 2-1/2-in. biscuit cutter.

Place biscuits over chicken mixture. Bake, uncovered, at 400° for 15-20 minutes or until biscuits are golden brown.

stan's smoky ribs

PREP: 70 min. | **GRILL:** 10 min. | **YIELD:** 4 servings.

You can't stop eating these tender, saucy ribs. When folks smell them cooking, they come running! STANLEY PICHON, SLIDELL, LOUISIANA

3	pounds bone-in country-style pork ribs
1/2	teaspoon garlic salt
1/2	teaspoon pepper
1	cup ketchup
1/2	cup packed brown sugar
1/2	cup molasses
1/4	cup spicy brown mustard
2	tablespoons Worcestershire sauce
1	tablespoon Liquid Smoke, optional
1/8	teaspoon cayenne pepper

Place ribs in a 5-qt. Dutch oven; cover with water. Add garlic salt and pepper; bring to a boil over medium heat. Reduce heat; cover and simmer for 1 hour.

Meanwhile, combine the remaining ingredients; set aside. Drain ribs. Grill, uncovered, over medium heat for 8-10 minutes or until meat is tender, basting several times with sauce. Serve remaining sauce with ribs.

stan's smoky ribs

old-fashioned chicken pot pie

PREP: 1 hour | **BAKE:** 15 min. | **YIELD:** 6-8 servings.

I always have leftover chicken broth on hand and use it in many dishes, including this comforting family favorite. Use my recipe to make homemade biscuits or simply purchase store-bought ones if you're pressed for time. LILIANE JAHNKE, CYPRESS, TEXAS

1-1/2	cups sliced fresh mushrooms
1	cup sliced fresh carrots
1/2	cup chopped onion
1/3	cup butter
1/3	cup all-purpose flour
1-1/2	cups chicken broth
1-1/2	cups milk
4	cups cubed cooked chicken breast
1	cup frozen peas
1	jar (2 ounces) diced pimientos, drained
1	teaspoon salt

BISCUIT TOPPING:

2	cups all-purpose flour
4	teaspoons baking powder
2	teaspoons sugar
1/2	teaspoon salt
1/2	teaspoon cream of tartar
1/2	cup cold butter, cubed
2/3	cup milk

In a large saucepan, saute the mushrooms, carrots and onion in butter until tender; sprinkle with flour. Gradually stir in broth and milk until blended. Bring to a boil; cook and stir for 2 minutes or until thickened. Add the chicken, peas, pimientos and salt ; heat through. Pour into a greased shallow 2-1/2-qt. baking dish; set aside.

tangy stuffed peppers

PREP: 20 min. | **BAKE:** 25 min. | **YIELD:** 4 servings.

My parents were farmers, so I've always liked to cook with fresh vegetables. This recipe represents our part of the country, since both green peppers and rice are grown here. It's one of my family's favorites. The Worcestershire sauce is what makes the filling tangy.

ROSIE WENDEL, BAY CITY, TEXAS

4	large green peppers
1	pound ground beef
1	small onion, chopped
1-1/2	cups cooked long grain rice
1/4	cup grated Parmesan cheese
6	teaspoons Worcestershire sauce, *divided*
1/2	teaspoon salt
1	can (15 ounces) tomato sauce
1/3	cup water

Additional Parmesan cheese, optional

Cut tops off peppers and remove seeds. Finely chop pepper tops; set aside. In a large saucepan, cook whole peppers in boiling water for 3-5 minutes. Drain and rinse in cold water; set aside.

In a large skillet, cook the beef, onion and chopped peppers over medium heat until meat is no longer pink and vegetables are tender; drain. Remove from the heat. Stir in the rice, Parmesan cheese, 4 teaspoons Worcestershire sauce and salt. Spoon into peppers.

Place in a greased 2-qt. baking dish. Combine the tomato sauce, water and remaining Worcestershire sauce; drizzle over peppers.

Cover and bake at 350° for 25-30 minutes or until the peppers are tender. Sprinkle with additional Parmesan cheese if desired.

smoky shrimp with creamy grits

PREP/TOTAL TIME: 30 min. | **YIELD:** 6 servings.

Chipotle peppers and fire-roasted tomatoes give this dish a smoky, spicy flavor, which is nicely balanced by creamy grits. The addition of shrimp makes it extra special. JO-ANNE COOPER, CAMROSE, ALBERTA

3	cups water
1	can (14-3/4 ounces) cream-style corn
1	teaspoon salt
3/4	cup quick-cooking grits
4	green onions, finely chopped
2	ounces cream cheese, softened
1/4	cup butter, cubed
1	large garlic clove, minced
1-1/2	pounds uncooked large shrimp, peeled and deveined
1	can (14-1/2 ounces) fire-roasted diced tomatoes, drained
1	teaspoon seafood seasoning
1	teaspoon minced chipotle pepper in adobo sauce

In a large saucepan, bring the water, corn and salt to a boil. Slowly stir in grits. Reduce heat; cook and stir for 5-7 minutes or until thickened. Remove from the heat; stir in onions and cream cheese.

In a large skillet, melt butter. Add garlic; saute for 1 minute. Add shrimp; cook and stir for 3-4 minutes or until shrimp turn pink. Stir in the tomatoes, seafood seasoning and chipotle pepper; heat through. Serve with grits.

chicken-fried steak

PREP/TOTAL TIME: 30 min. | **YIELD:** 4 servings.

We raise cattle on our ranch, so beef is a mainstay at our house. I adapted this dish to cut out a lot of the fat and calories found in traditional steak. My family loves this lighter version just as much.

CAROL DALE, GREENVILLE, TEXAS

3/4	cup all-purpose flour
1/4	teaspoon pepper
1	pound beef round steak, cut into serving-size pieces
1/2	cup fat-free milk
2	tablespoons canola oil

GRAVY:

2	tablespoons water
4-1/2	teaspoons all-purpose flour
3/4	cup fat-free milk
1/8	teaspoon pepper

In a shallow bowl, combine flour and pepper. Add beef; turn to coat. Remove meat and pound with a mallet to tenderize. Pour milk into another shallow bowl. Heat oil in a skillet. Dip meat in milk, then coat again in flour mixture; add to skillet. Cover and cook over low heat for 10 minutes on each side or until meat is no longer pink. Remove and keep warm.

For gravy, add water to skillet; stir to loosen browned bits from pan. In a small bowl, combine the flour, milk and pepper until smooth. Gradually stir into skillet. Bring to a boil; cook and stir for 1-2 minutes or until thickened. Serve with steak.

country fried chicken

PREP: 20 min. | **COOK:** 40 min. | **YIELD:** 4 servings.

Country fried chicken is classic picnic fare. We like to eat it cold, alongside a tossed salad and watermelon slices. It's a real treat!
REBEKAH MILLER, ROCKY MOUNT, VIRGINIA

1	**cup all-purpose flour**
2	**teaspoons garlic salt**
2	**teaspoons pepper**
1	**teaspoon paprika**
1/2	**teaspoon poultry seasoning**
1	**egg**
1/2	**cup milk**
1	**broiler/fryer chicken (3 to 3-1/2 pounds), cut up**

Oil for frying

In a large resealable plastic bag, combine the flour and seasonings. In a shallow bowl, beat egg and milk. Dip chicken pieces into egg mixture, then add to bag, a few pieces at a time, and shake to coat.

In a large skillet, heat 1/4 in. of oil; fry chicken in oil until browned on all sides. Cover and simmer for 35-40 minutes or until juices run clear and chicken is tender, turning occasionally. Uncover and cook 5 minutes longer. Drain on paper towels.

country fried chicken

salisbury steak deluxe

salisbury steak deluxe

PREP/TOTAL TIME: 30 min. | **YIELD:** 6 servings.

Give my recipe for salisbury steak a try, and I promise you won't be disappointed! I had to search a long time to find one that pleased my palate. It's handy, too, because it can be prepared in advance and stored in the fridge until ready to serve.
DENISE BARTEET, SHREVEPORT, LOUISIANA

1	**can (10-3/4 ounces) condensed cream of mushroom soup, undiluted**
1	**tablespoon prepared mustard**
2	**teaspoons Worcestershire sauce**
1	**teaspoon prepared horseradish**
1	**egg**
1/4	**cup dry bread crumbs**
1/4	**cup finely chopped onion**
1/2	**teaspoon salt**

Dash pepper

1-1/2	**pound ground beef**
1	**to 2 tablespoons canola oil**
1/2	**cup water**
2	**tablespoons chopped fresh parsley**

In a small bowl, combine the soup, mustard, Worcestershire sauce and horseradish. Set aside. In another bowl, lightly beat the egg. Add the bread crumbs, onion, salt, pepper and 1/4 cup of the soup mixture. Crumble beef over mixture and mix well. Shape into six patties.

In a large skillet, brown the patties in oil; drain. Combine remaining soup mixture with water; pour over patties. Cover and cook over low heat for 10-15 minutes or until meat is no longer pink and a meat thermometer reads 160°. Remove patties to a serving platter; serve sauce with meat. Sprinkle with parsley.

74

78

79

81

BENEDICT EGGS IN PASTRY

breakfast & brunch

benedict eggs in pastry

PREP: 30 min. **| BAKE:** 20 min. **| YIELD:** 4 servings.

Here's a new twist on an old favorite. Inside these puffy, golden bundles is an omelet-like filling of eggs, ham, cheese and a lemony hollandaise sauce.

CATHY SLUSSLER, MAGNOLIA, TEXAS

2	egg yolks
2	tablespoons lemon juice
1	teaspoon Dijon mustard
1/2	cup butter, melted

Dash cayenne pepper

2	cups cubed fully cooked ham
2	green onions, chopped
1	tablespoon butter
6	eggs, lightly beaten
2	tablespoons 2% milk
1	package (17.3 ounces) frozen puff pastry, thawed
1	cup (4 ounces) shredded cheddar cheese
1	egg
1	tablespoon water

Minced fresh tarragon, optional

In a double boiler over simmering water or a small heavy saucepan, constantly whisk the egg yolks, lemon juice and mustard until mixture begins to thicken and reaches 160°. Reduce heat to low. Slowly drizzle in warm melted butter, whisking constantly. Whisk in cayenne.

Transfer to a small bowl if necessary. Place bowl in a larger bowl of warm water. Keep warm, stirring occasionally, until ready to use.

In a large skillet over medium heat, cook and stir ham and onions in butter until onions are tender. In a large bowl, whisk six eggs and milk. Add egg mixture to the pan; cook and stir until set. Remove from the heat; stir in 1/3 cup reserved hollandaise sauce. Set aside.

On a lightly floured surface, unfold puff pastry. Roll each sheet into a 12-in. x 9-1/2-in. rectangle; cut each in half widthwise. Place 1 cup egg mixture on half of each rectangle; sprinkle with cheese.

Beat egg and water; brush over pastry edges. Bring an opposite corner of pastry over the egg mixture; pinch seams to seal. With a small sharp knife, cut several slits in the top.

Transfer to a greased baking sheet; brush with remaining egg mixture. Bake at 400° for 18-22 minutes or until golden brown. Serve with remaining hollandaise sauce. Sprinkle with tarragon if desired.

apple fritters

PREP: 15 min. **| COOK:** 30 min. **| YIELD:** 40 fritters.

My kids love these fritters year-round, but I get even more requests in the fall when there are plenty of apples in season. I like to serve them as a special breakfast treat when we host overnight guests.

KATIE BEECHY, SEYMOUR, MISSOURI

2-1/2	cups all-purpose flour
1/2	cup nonfat dry milk powder
1/3	cup sugar
2	teaspoons baking powder
1	teaspoon salt
2	eggs
1	cup water
2	cups chopped peeled apples

Oil for deep-fat frying

Sugar

In a large bowl, combine first five ingredients. Whisk eggs and water; add to dry ingredients just until moistened. Fold in apples.

In an electric skillet, heat oil to 375°. Drop batter by teaspoonfuls, a few at a time, in hot oil. Fry until golden brown, about 1-1/2 minutes on each side. Drain on paper towels. Roll warm fritters in sugar. Serve warm.

apple fritters

southern twist

To add even more Southern flair to Benedict Eggs in Pastry, replace the ham with shrimp. Simply peel and devein about 1 pound raw medium shrimp. Add shrimp and 1 teaspoon salt to 3 quarts boiling water. Reduce heat and simmer, uncovered, for 1 to 3 minutes or until the shrimp turn pink. Watch closely to avoid overcooking. Drain immediately. Chop the shrimp and add approximately 2 cups in place of the cubed cooked ham called for in the recipe.

sweet potato waffles with nut topping

In a large bowl, combine the biscuit mix, brown sugar and spices. In another bowl, whisk the egg, milk, sweet potatoes, oil and vanilla. Stir into dry ingredients just until combined.

Bake in a preheated waffle iron according to manufacturer's directions until golden brown.

Meanwhile, in a small skillet, melt butter over medium heat. Add pecans and walnuts. Cook and stir for 2 minutes. Add the brown sugar, water, cinnamon, salt and nutmeg. Cook and stir until sugar is dissolved. Serve waffles with topping and syrup.

spicy sausage patties

PREP/TOTAL TIME: 20 min. | **YIELD:** 4 servings.

Jazz up any breakfast with these subtly spiced sausage patties. They take only 20 minutes to make and are guaranteed to perk up your taste buds. ATHENA RUSSELL, FLORENCE, SOUTH CAROLINA

- 1/2 teaspoon salt
- 1/2 teaspoon dried sage leaves
- 1/4 teaspoon ground coriander
- 1/4 teaspoon pepper
- 1/8 to 1/4 teaspoon crushed red pepper flakes
- 3/4 pound ground pork

In a large bowl, combine the first five ingredients. Crumble pork over mixture and mix well. Shape into four 3-in. patties.

In a large skillet, cook patties over medium heat for 5-6 minutes on each side or until meat is no longer pink. Drain on paper towels.

sweet potato waffles with nut topping

PREP: 20 min. | **COOK:** 5 min./batch | **YIELD:** 12 waffles.

Ready in just minutes, these tender waffles have a wonderfully sweet and crunchy topping. They're a mouthwatering way to get your family out of bed in the morning. CHRISTINE KEATING, NORWALK, CALIFORNIA

- 2 cups biscuit/baking mix
- 2 tablespoons brown sugar
- 1/2 teaspoon ground cinnamon
- 1/4 teaspoon ground ginger
- 1/4 teaspoon ground nutmeg
- 1 egg
- 1-1/3 cups 2% milk
- 1 cup canned sweet potatoes, mashed
- 2 tablespoons canola oil
- 1 teaspoon vanilla extract

TOPPING:
- 1 tablespoon butter
- 1/2 cup chopped pecans
- 1/2 cup chopped walnuts
- 2 tablespoons brown sugar
- 1 tablespoon water
- 1/8 teaspoon ground cinnamon

spicy sausage patties

sausage johnnycake

PREP: 20 min. | **BAKE:** 35 min. | **YIELD:** 6 servings.

Here's a hearty breakfast with plenty of old-fashioned Southern flavor. I serve this specialty to my bed-and-breakfast customers. The cake's savory middle and maple syrup topping always garner compliments.

LORRAINE GUYN, CALGARY, ALBERTA

1	cup cornmeal
2	cups buttermilk
12	uncooked breakfast sausage links
1-1/3	cups all-purpose flour
1/4	cup sugar
1-1/2	teaspoons baking powder
1/2	teaspoon baking soda
1/2	teaspoon salt
1/3	cup shortening
1	eggs, lightly beaten
1/2	teaspoon vanilla extract

Maple syrup

In a small bowl, combine cornmeal and buttermilk; let stand for 10 minutes.

Meanwhile, in a large skillet over medium heat, cook sausage until no longer pink; drain on paper towels. Arrange eight links in a spoke-like pattern in a greased 9-in. deep-dish pie plate. Cut the remaining links in half; place halves between whole sausages.

In a large bowl, combine the flour, sugar, baking powder, baking soda and salt. Cut in shortening until mixture resembles coarse crumbs.

Stir egg and vanilla into cornmeal mixture; add to the dry ingredients and stir just until blended. Pour the batter over the sausages.

Bake at 400° for 35-40 minutes or until a toothpick inserted near the center comes out clean. Serve warm with syrup.

blueberry-stuffed french toast

PREP: 35 min. | **BAKE:** 15 min. | **YIELD:** 8 servings.

This luscious recipe lets you enjoy sweetened blueberries sandwiched between French toast slices drizzled with a decadent berry-citrus sauce. MYRNA KOLDENHOVEN, SANBORN, IOWA

1-1/2	cups fresh *or* frozen blueberries
3	tablespoons sugar, *divided*
8	slices Italian bread (1-1/4 inches thick)
4	eggs, lightly beaten
1/2	cup orange juice
1	teaspoon grated orange peel

Dash salt

BLUEBERRY ORANGE SAUCE:

3	tablespoons sugar
1	tablespoon cornstarch
1/8	teaspoon salt
1/4	cup orange juice
1/4	cup water
1-1/2	cups orange segments
1	cup fresh *or* frozen blueberries
1/3	cup sliced almonds

In a small bowl, combine the blueberries and 2 tablespoons sugar. Cut a pocket in the side of each slice of Italian bread.

blueberry-stuffed french toast

Fill each pocket with about 3 tablespoons of the blueberry-sugar mixture.

In a shallow bowl, whisk the eggs, orange juice, orange peel, salt and remaining sugar. Carefully dip both sides of bread in egg mixture (do not squeeze out filling). Place in a greased 15-in. x 10-in. x 1-in. baking pan. Bake at 400° for 7-1/2 minutes on each side; turning gently.

Meanwhile, in a small saucepan, combine the sugar, cornstarch and salt. Gently whisk in orange juice and water until smooth. Bring to a boil; cook and stir for 1-2 minutes or until thickened. Reduce heat; stir in oranges and blueberries. Cook for 5 minutes or until heated through. Serve with French toast; sprinkle with almonds.

ham griddle cakes

PREP/TOTAL TIME: 30 min. | **YIELD:** 8 pancakes.

If you're looking for a new way to use up leftover ham, give these golden pancakes a whirl. I serve them on special occasions, and I'm always asked for the recipe. VIRGINIA CULLEN, SARASOTA, FLORIDA

1	cup all-purpose flour
1-1/2	teaspoons baking powder
2	eggs
3/4	cup milk
1	cup ground fully cooked ham

Pancake syrup

In a large bowl, combine flour and baking powder. In another bowl, beat the eggs and milk. Stir into dry ingredients just until moistened. Fold in ham.

Pour the batter by 1/4 cupfuls onto a lightly greased hot griddle. Turn when bubbles form on top. Cook until the second side is golden brown. Serve with syrup.

mom's fried apples

PREP: 5 min. | **COOK:** 30 min. | **YIELD:** 6-8 servings.

This recipe was one of my mom's specialties. The aroma of these tender apples reminds me of home. MARGIE TAPPE, PRAGUE, OKLAHOMA

1/2	cup butter, cubed
6	medium unpeeled tart red apples, sliced
3/4	cup sugar, *divided*
3/4	teaspoon ground cinnamon

Melt butter in a large skillet. Add apples and 1/2 cup sugar; stir to mix well. Cover and cook over low heat for 20 minutes or until apples are tender, stirring frequently.

Add cinnamon and remaining sugar. Cook and stir over medium-high heat for 10 minutes or until apples are tender.

biscuits and sausage gravy

biscuits and sausage gravy

PREP/TOTAL TIME: 15 min. | **YIELD:** 2 servings.

Take your taste buds on a "trip" to the South with this traditional recipe. Over the years, I've adapted it to suit my family's tastes.

SUE BAKER, JONESBORO, ARKANSAS

1/4	pound bulk pork sausage
2	tablespoons butter
2	to 3 tablespoons all-purpose flour
1/4	teaspoon salt
1/8	teaspoon pepper
1-1/4	to 1-1/3 cups milk

Warm biscuits

In a small skillet, cook sausage over medium heat until no longer pink; drain. Add butter and heat until melted. Add the flour, salt and pepper; cook and stir until blended. Gradually add the milk, stirring constantly. Bring to a boil; cook and stir for 2 minutes or until thickened. Serve with biscuits.

tex-mex defined

"Tex-Mex" is a term used to describe a cuisine that combines foods available in the United States with dishes that are strongly influenced by the cuisines of Mexico. Tex-Mex is most famous in Texas, but popularity of this regional cuisine has spread to other states, particularly those in the Southwest.

tex-mex cheese strata

PREP: 15 min. + chilling | **BAKE:** 40 min. + standing
YIELD: 6-8 servings.

Tortilla chips add a little fun to this south-of-the-border dish. To satisfy those who prefer a spicy kick, substitute pepper Jack cheese for the Monterey Jack.

VICKIE LOWREY, FALLON, NEVADA

4	cups coarsely crushed nacho tortilla chips
2	cups (8 ounces) shredded Monterey Jack cheese
1	small onion, finely chopped
1	tablespoon butter
6	eggs, lightly beaten
2-1/2	cups milk
1	can (4 ounces) chopped green chilies, undrained
3	tablespoons ketchup
1/4	teaspoon hot pepper sauce

Arrange tortilla chips in a greased 13-in. x 9-in. baking dish; sprinkle with cheese and set aside. In a large skillet, saute onion in butter until tender.

In a large bowl, whisk the eggs, milk, onion, chilies, ketchup and hot pepper sauce; pour over cheese. Cover and refrigerate overnight.

Remove from the refrigerator 30 minutes before baking. Bake, uncovered, at 350° for 40-45 minutes until a knife inserted near the center comes out clean. Let stand for 5 minutes before cutting.

tex-mex cheese strata

new orleans beignets

PREP: 15 min. | **COOK:** 35 min. | **YIELD:** 4 dozen.

These sweet French doughnuts are square instead of round and don't have a hole in the middle. They're a traditional part of breakfast in New Orleans.

BETH DAWSON, JACKSON, LOUISIANA

1	package (1/4 ounce) active dry yeast
1/4	cup warm water (110° to 115°)
1	cup evaporated milk
1/2	cup canola oil
1/4	cup sugar
1	egg
4-1/2	cups self-rising flour

Oil for deep-fat frying

Confectioners' sugar

In a large bowl, dissolve yeast in warm water. Add the milk, oil, sugar and egg and 2 cups flour. Beat until smooth. Stir in enough remaining flour to form a soft dough (dough will be sticky). Do not knead. Cover and refrigerate overnight.

Punch dough down. Turn onto a floured surface; roll into a 16-in. x 12-in. rectangle. Cut into 2-in. squares.

In an electric skillet or deep-fat fryer, heat oil to 375°. Fry squares, a few at a time, until golden brown on both sides. Drain squares on paper towels. Roll warm beignets in confectioners' sugar.

EDITOR'S NOTE: As a substitute for each cup of self-rising flour, place 1-1/2 teaspoons baking powder and 1/2 teaspoon salt in a measuring cup. Add all-purpose flour to measure 1 cup.

southwestern omelet

PREP/TOTAL TIME: 20 min. | **YIELD:** 4 servings.

Southwestern flavors add a little spark to the eggs in this recipe. Even though we live in the Northwest, we can't seem to get enough!

PATRICIA COLLINS, IMBLER, OREGON

1/2	cup chopped onion
1	jalapeno pepper, minced
1	tablespoon canola oil
6	egg, lightly beaten
6	bacon strips, cooked and crumbled
1	small tomato, chopped
1	ripe avocado, cut into 1-inch slices
1	cup (4 ounces) shredded Monterey Jack cheese, *divided*

Salt and pepper to taste

Salsa, optional

In a large skillet, saute the onion and jalapeno in oil until tender; remove with a slotted spoon and set aside. Pour the eggs into the same skillet; cover and cook over low heat for 3-4 minutes.

Sprinkle with the onion mixture, bacon, tomato, avocado and 1/2 cup cheese. Season with salt and pepper.

Fold omelet in half over filling. Cover and cook for 3-4 minutes or until eggs are set. Sprinkle with remaining cheese. Serve with salsa if desired.

EDITOR'S NOTE: We recommend wearing disposable gloves when cutting hot peppers. Avoid touching your face.

southwestern omelet

fried potatoes

PREP/TOTAL TIME: 15 min. | **YIELD:** 3-4 servings.

Fried potatoes are a family favorite. The recipe takes just minutes to make and is a wonderful way to use up leftover spuds. Enjoy them as part of a hearty breakfast or as a side to your favorite dinner entree.

TASTE OF HOME TEST KITCHEN

3	cups diced cooked potatoes
1/2	cup diced cooked onion
2	tablespoons butter

Salt and pepper to taste

In a large skillet, cook potatoes and onion in butter over medium heat for 10 minutes or until golden brown. Season with salt and pepper.

buttermilk pecan pancakes

PREP/TOTAL TIME: 25 min. | **YIELD:** 16 pancakes.

With crunchy pecans in each bite, these light, fluffy pancakes make an delightful morning entree. Add sliced apples and whipped cream on top to make them extra indulgent.

JANN BRAUN, CHATHAM, ILLINOIS

3	eggs, *separated*
3	tablespoons butter, melted
1-1/2	cups all-purpose flour
1/2	to 1 cup chopped pecans
1	tablespoon sugar
1	teaspoon baking powder
1	teaspoon baking soda
1/2	teaspoon salt
1-2/3	cups buttermilk

In a large bowl, beat egg yolks and butter. Combine the flour, pecans, sugar, baking powder, baking soda and salt; add to the egg mixture alternately with buttermilk. Beat egg whites until stiff peaks form; fold into batter.

Pour batter by 1/4 cupfuls onto a lightly greased hot griddle; turn when bubbles form on top of pancakes. Cook until second side is golden brown.

out of buttermilk?

There's no need to run to the store if you've run out of buttermilk. Instead, make your own easy substitute. For each cup of buttermilk, use 1 tablespoon of white vinegar or lemon juice plus enough milk to measure 1 cup. Stir, then let stand for 5 minutes. You can also use 1 cup of plain yogurt or 1-3/4 teaspoons cream of tartar plus 1 cup milk.

ham and leek pies

PREP: 40 min. | **BAKE:** 20 min. | **YIELD:** 4 servings.

This is my favorite recipe for leftover ham. I freeze the individual dishes and pull one out whenever I need a quick meal. BONNY TILLMAN, ACWORTH, GEORGIA

4	cups sliced leeks (white portion only)
1/2	pound sliced fresh mushrooms
1-1/2	cups sliced fresh carrots
1/4	cup butter, cubed
1/2	cup all-purpose flour
1-1/4	cups vegetable broth
1-1/4	cups milk
1-3/4	cups diced fully cooked ham
2	tablespoons minced fresh parsley
1/4	to 1/2 teaspoon ground nutmeg

Dash pepper

1	sheet frozen puff pastry, thawed
1	egg, lightly beaten

In a large saucepan, saute the leeks, mushrooms and carrots in butter until tender. Stir in flour until blended. Gradually stir in broth and milk. Bring to a boil over medium heat. Cook and stir for 2 minutes or until thickened. Remove from the heat; stir in the ham, parsley, nutmeg and pepper.

On a lightly floured surface, roll puff pastry to 1/4-in. thickness. Using a 10-oz. ramekin as a template, cut out four tops for pies.

Fill four greased 10-oz. ramekins with leek mixture; top with pastry. Cut slits in pastry. Cut decorative shapes out of pastry scraps if desired; arrange over pies. Brush tops with egg.

Bake at 425° for 18-22 minutes or until golden brown. Let stand for 5 minutes before serving.

ham and leek pies

jelly doughnuts

jelly doughnuts

PREP: 25 min. + rising | **COOK:** 30 min. | **YIELD:** 2-1/2 dozen.

After the first tender bite, folks will be licking sugar from their fingers and asking you for seconds of these colossal jelly-filled treats. The doughnuts are best served warm.
LEE BREMSON, KANSAS CITY, MISSOURI

2	packages (1/4 ounce *each*) active dry yeast
2	cups warm milk (110° to 115°)
7	cups all-purpose flour, *divided*
4	egg yolks
1	egg
1/2	cup sugar
1	teaspoon salt
2	teaspoons grated lemon peel
1/2	teaspoon vanilla extract
1/2	cup butter, melted

Oil for deep-fat frying

Red jelly of your choice

Additional sugar

In a large bowl, dissolve yeast in warm milk. Add 2 cups flour; mix well. Let stand in a warm place for 30 minutes. Add the egg yolks, egg, sugar, salt, lemon peel and vanilla; mix well. Beat in butter and remaining flour. Do not knead. Cover and let rise in a warm place until doubled, about 45 minutes.

Punch dough down. On a lightly floured surface, roll out to 1/2 in. thickness. Cut with a 2-1/2-in. biscuit cutter. Place on a lightly greased baking sheets. Cover and let rise until nearly doubled, about 35 minutes.

In a deep-fat fryer or electric skillet, heat oil to 375°. Fry doughnuts, a few at a time, for 1-1/2 to 2 minutes on each side or until browned. Drain on paper towels.

Cool for 2-3 minutes; cut a small slit with a sharp knife on one side of each doughnut. Cut a small hole in the corner of a pastry or plastic bag; insert a very small round tip. Fill with jelly. Fill each doughnut with about 1 teaspoon jelly. Carefully roll warm doughnuts in sugar. Serve warm.

sunshine crepes

PREP: 15 min. + chilling | **COOK:** 15 min. | **YIELD:** 6 servings.

My hungry clan requested a light breakfast one morning, so I whipped up these sweet and fruity crepes. They were a big hit!

MARY HOBBS, CAMPBELL, MISSOURI

2/3	cup milk	
2	eggs	
1	tablespoon canola oil	
1/2	cup all-purpose flour	
1	teaspoon sugar	
1/4	teaspoon salt	

FILLING:

1	can (20 ounces) crushed pineapple, drained	
1	can (11 ounces) mandarin oranges, drained	
1	teaspoon vanilla extract	
1	carton (8 ounces) frozen whipped topping, thawed	

Confectioners' sugar

In a large bowl, beat the milk, eggs and oil. Combine the flour, sugar and salt; add to milk mixture and mix well. Cover and refrigerate for 1 hour.

Coat an 8-in. nonstick skillet with cooking spray; heat over medium heat. Stir crepe batter; pour 2 tablespoons into center of skillet. Lift and tilt pan to coat bottom evenly. Cook until top appears dry; turn and cook 15-20 seconds longer. Remove to a wire rack. Repeat with remaining batter, coating skillet as needed. When cool, stack crepes with waxed paper or paper towels in between.

For filling, in a large bowl, combine the pineapple, oranges and vanilla; fold in whipped topping. Spoon 1/3 cup down the center of each crepe; roll up. Dust with confectioners' sugar.

sunshine crepes

tropical fruit salad

PREP/TOTAL TIME: 25 min. | **YIELD:** 8 servings.

This recipe makes an excellent breakfast or dessert. Toasted coconut and a medley of fresh fruits bring the flavors of the tropics indoors.

KATIE COVINGTON, BLACKSBURG, SOUTH CAROLINA

1	medium mango, peeled and cubed
1	medium green apple, cubed
1	medium red apple, cubed
1	medium pear, cubed
1	medium navel orange, peeled and chopped
2	medium kiwifruit, peeled and chopped
10	seedless red grapes, halved
2	tablespoons orange juice
1	firm medium banana, sliced
1/4	cup flaked coconut, toasted

In a large bowl, combine the first seven ingredients. Drizzle with orange juice; toss gently to coat. Refrigerate until serving. Just before serving, fold in banana and sprinkle salad with coconut.

mango primer

When purchasing mangoes, look for ones with unblemished green to yellow skin tinged with red. Ripe mangoes will feel fairly firm when gently pressed and have a sweet, fruity aroma.

Keep green mangoes at room temperature out of direct sunlight until ripened. When ripe, they can be refrigerated for 5 days.

SOUTHERN SWEET POTATO PIE

cakes & pies

southern sweet potato pie

PREP: 15 min. | **BAKE:** 55 min. + chilling | **YIELD:** 8 servings.

This recipe is very popular in the South. It's a particular favorite at our house because we always have plenty of sweet potatoes in our garden. Try it with a dollop of whipped cream on top.
BONNIE HOLCOMB, FULTON, MISSISSIPPI

3	tablespoons all-purpose flour
1-2/3	cups sugar
1/4	teaspoon ground nutmeg
Pinch salt	
1	cup mashed sweet potatoes
2	eggs
1/4	cup light corn syrup
1/2	cup butter, softened
3/4	cup evaporated milk
1	unbaked pastry shell (9 inches)

In a small bowl, combine the flour, sugar, nutmeg and salt. In a large bowl, beat the potatoes, eggs, corn syrup, butter and sugar mixture. Gradually stir in milk. Pour into pastry shell.

Bake at 350° for 55-60 minutes. Cool on a wire rack for 1 hour. Refrigerate for at least 3 hours before serving. Refrigerate leftovers.

lemonade icebox pie

PREP: 15 min. + chilling | **YIELD:** 8 servings.

You will detect a definite lemonade flavor in this refreshing pie. This high and fluffy dessert has a smooth consistency everyone will love.
CHERYL WILT, EGLON, WEST VIRGINIA

1	package (8 ounces) cream cheese, softened
1	can (14 ounces) sweetened condensed milk
3/4	cup thawed lemonade concentrate
1	carton (8 ounces) frozen whipped topping, thawed
Yellow food coloring, optional	
1	graham cracker crust (9 inches)

whipped cream

In most recipes, whipped cream may be used instead of whipped topping. But be aware that there may be some differences in texture and stability, which could result in minor changes in the end product. When substituting, keep in mind that whipping cream doubles once it is whipped. If a recipe calls for an 8-ounce carton of whipped topping, whip 1-1/2 cups of whipping cream, which will yield 3 cups.

In a large bowl, beat cream cheese and milk until smooth. Beat in lemonade concentrate. Fold in whipped topping and food coloring if desired. Pour into crust. Cover and refrigerate until set.

deep-fried cherry pies

PREP/TOTAL TIME: 30 min. | **YIELD:** 4 servings.

With a delightfully flaky crust, these stuffed cherry pies always make a quick dessert. My family loves them after dinner or as a snack, but they're also wonderful for an on-the-go lunch.
MONICA LARKIN, SHINNSTON, WEST VIRGINIA

1	cup all-purpose flour
1/4	teaspoon baking powder
1/4	teaspoon salt
2	tablespoons shortening
1/3	cup boiling water
1	cup cherry pie filling
Oil for deep-fat frying	
1/4	cup maple syrup
1/4	cup whipped topping

In a small bowl, combine the flour, baking powder and salt. Cut in shortening until mixture resembles coarse crumbs. Stir in water just until moistened. Turn onto a lightly floured surface; knead 8-10 times.

Divide dough into four portions; roll each into an 8-in. circle. Place 1/4 cup of pie filling in the center of each circle. Fold dough over filling; secure with toothpicks.

In an electric skillet or deep fat-fryer, heat 1 in. of oil to 375°. Fry pies, folded side down, in oil for 2-3 minutes or until lightly browned. Turn and fry 2-3 minutes longer. Drain on paper towels. Remove toothpicks. Serve with syrup and whipped topping.

deep-fried cherry pies

italian cream cheese cake

PREP: 40 min. | **BAKE:** 20 min. + cooling | **YIELD:** 12 servings.

Buttermilk makes every bite of this awesome dessert moist and flavorful. I rely on this recipe year-round.
JOYCE LUTZ, CENTERVIEW, MISSOURI

1/2	cup butter, softened
1/2	cup shortening
2	cups sugar
5	eggs, *separated*
1	teaspoon vanilla extract
2	cups all-purpose flour
1	teaspoon baking soda
1	cup buttermilk
1-1/2	cups flaked coconut
1	cup chopped pecans

CREAM CHEESE FROSTING:

2	packages (one 8 ounces, one 3 ounces) cream cheese, softened
3/4	cup butter, softened
6	cups confectioners' sugar
1-1/2	teaspoons vanilla extract
3/4	cup chopped pecans

In a large bowl, cream the butter, shortening and sugar until light and fluffy. Beat in egg yolks and vanilla. Combine flour and baking soda; add to creamed mixture alternately with buttermilk. Beat just until combined. Stir in the coconut and pecans.

In a small bowl, beat egg whites until stiff peaks form. Fold a fourth of the egg whites into batter, then fold in remaining whites. Pour into three greased and floured 9-in. round baking pans.

Bake at 350° for 20-25 minutes or until a toothpick inserted near the center comes out clean. Cool for 10 minutes before removing the cakes from pans to wire racks to cool completely.

In a large bowl, beat cream cheese and butter until smooth. Beat in confectioners' sugar and vanilla until fluffy. Stir in pecans. Spread frosting between layers and over top and sides of cake. Store in the refrigerator.

classic red velvet cake

PREP: 25 min. | **BAKE:** 20 min. + cooling | **YIELD:** 12 servings.

This ruby-red cake with its lovely cream cheese frosting has become my signature dessert. I can't go to any family function without it. The cake has a buttery, chocolate taste.

KATIE SLOAN, CHARLOTTE, NORTH CAROLINA

1/2	cup shortening
1-1/2	cups sugar
2	eggs
1	bottle (1 ounce) red food coloring
3	teaspoons white vinegar
1	teaspoon butter flavoring
1	teaspoon vanilla extract
2-1/2	cups cake flour
1/4	cup baking cocoa
1	teaspoon baking soda
1	teaspoon salt
1	cup buttermilk

FROSTING:

1	package (8 ounces) cream cheese, softened
1/2	cup butter, softened
3-3/4	cups confectioners' sugar
3	teaspoons vanilla extract

In a large bowl, cream shortening and sugar until light fluffy. Add eggs, one at a time, beating well after each addition. Beat in the food coloring, vinegar, butter flavoring and vanilla. Combine the flour, cocoa, baking soda and salt; add to creamed mixture alternately with buttermilk, beating well after each addition.

Pour into three greased and floured 9-in. round baking pans. Bake at 350° for 20-25 minutes or until a toothpick inserted near the center comes out clean. Cool for 10 minutes before removing from pans to wire racks to cool completely.

In a large bowl, combine frosting ingredients; beat until smooth and creamy. Spread between layers and over top and sides of cake.

cake flour

Cake flour is often used in layer cakes when a fine, tender crumb is desired. Made from soft wheat, cake flour contains about 8 to 10% protein. All-purpose flour is made from hard wheat and contains about 10 to 12% protein. Flour with a lower percentage of protein will result in a cake that has a more delicate crumb. Cake flour is also more finely ground and has undergone a bleaching process, so it will produce a cake with a finer crumb than all-purpose flour. All-purpose flour will still yield a moist cake, but the texture won't be as fine.

old-fashioned coconut pie

PREP: 20 min. | **BAKE:** 15 min. + cooling | **YIELD:** 6-8 servings.

My husband says it's not good cooking unless it's made from scratch. This recipe for coconut pie is an old-fashioned way to achieve just that.

BARBARA SMITH, FRANKLIN, GEORGIA

1	cup sugar
1/4	cup all-purpose flour
Dash salt	
3	eggs, lightly beaten
2	cups milk
1-1/2	teaspoons vanilla extract
1-1/4	cups flaked coconut, *divided*
1	pie shell (9 inches), baked

MERINGUE:

3	egg whites
6	tablespoons sugar

In a large saucepan, combine the sugar, flour and salt. Combine egg yolks and milk; stir into dry ingredients until smooth. Cook and stir over medium heat until mixture is thickened and bubbly. Reduce heat to low; cook and stir 2 minutes longer. Remove from the heat; stir in vanilla and 1 cup coconut. Pour hot filling into pie shell.

For meringue, beat egg whites in a bowl until soft peaks form. Gradually beat in sugar until mixture forms stiff glossy peaks and sugar is dissolved. Spread meringue over hot filling. Sprinkle with remaining coconut.

Bake at 350° for 12-15 minutes or until golden. Cool. Store in the refrigerator.

old-fashioned coconut pie

apple pear cake

PREP: 25 min. | **BAKE:** 1 hour | **YIELD:** 12-15 servings.

My sister treated me to a delightfully moist apple cake, and I just had to have the recipe. When I made it myself, I tossed in some pears. Now every time I make it, people want to learn my secret!

MARY ANN LEES, CENTREVILLE, ALABAMA

2	cups shredded peeled tart apple
2	cups shredded peeled pears
2	cups sugar
1-1/4	cups canola oil
1	cup raisins
1	cup chopped pecans
2	eggs, lightly beaten
1	teaspoon vanilla extract
3	cups all-purpose flour
2	teaspoons baking soda
2	teaspoons ground cinnamon
1/2	teaspoon ground nutmeg
1/2	teaspoon salt

CREAM CHEESE FROSTING:

1	package (3 ounces) cream cheese, softened
3	cups confectioners' sugar
1/4	cup butter, softened
2	tablespoons milk
1/2	teaspoon vanilla extract

In a large bowl, combine the first eight ingredients. Combine dry ingredients; stir into the fruit mixture.

Pour into a greased 13-in. x 9-in. baking pan. Bake at 325° for 1 hour or until a toothpick inserted near the center comes out clean. Cool on a wire rack.

apple pear cake

mississippi mud cake

For frosting, in a large bowl, beat the cream cheese, confectioners' and butter until smooth. Beat in the milk and vanilla; frost cake. Store in the refrigerator.

mississippi mud cake

PREP: 20 min. | **BAKE:** 35 min. + cooling | **YIELD:** 16-20 servings.

Make this tempting cake, and you'll satisfy kids of all ages! A fudgy brownie-like base is topped with marshmallow creme and a nutty frosting. Everyone will be happy when you serve up big slices with glasses of cold milk or steaming mugs of coffee.

TAMMI SIMPSON, GREENSBURG, KENTUCKY

1	cup butter, softened
2	cups sugar
4	eggs
1-1/2	cups self-rising flour
1/2	cup baking cocoa
1	cup chopped pecans
1	jar (7 ounces) marshmallow creme

FROSTING:

1/2	cup butter, softened
3-3/4	cups confectioners' sugar
3	tablespoons baking cocoa
1	tablespoon vanilla extract
4	to 5 tablespoons 2% milk
1	cup chopped pecans

In a large bowl, cream butter and sugar until light and fluffy. Add eggs, one at a time, beating well after each addition. Combine flour and cocoa; gradually add to creamed mixture until blended. Fold in the pecans.

Transfer to a greased 13-in. x 9-in. baking pan. Bake at 350° for 35-40 minutes or until a toothpick inserted near the center comes out clean. Cool for 3 minutes (cake will fall in the center). Spoon the marshmallow creme over cake; carefully spread to cover top. Cool completely.

For frosting, in a small bowl, cream butter and confectioners' sugar until light and fluffy. Beat in the cocoa, vanilla and enough milk to achieve frosting consistency. Fold in pecans. Spread over marshmallow creme layer. Store in the refrigerator.

EDITOR'S NOTE: As a substitute for 1-1/2 cups self-rising flour, place 2-1/4 teaspoons baking powder and 3/4 teaspoon salt in a measuring cup. Add all-purpose flour to measure 1 cup. Combine with an additional 1/2 cup all-purpose flour.

old-time buttermilk pie

PREP: 15 min. | **BAKE:** 45 min. + cooling | **YIELD:** 8-10 servings.

This recipe is older than I am...and I was born in 1919! My mother and grandmother made this pie with buttermilk and eggs from our farm and set it on the tables at church meetings and social gatherings. I did the same and now my children make it, too!

KATE MATHEWS, SHREVEPORT, LOUISIANA

CRUST:

1-1/2	cups all-purpose flour
1	teaspoon salt
1/2	cup shortening
1/4	cup cold milk
1	egg, lightly beaten

FILLING:

1/2	cup butter
2	cups sugar
3	tablespoons all-purpose flour
3	eggs
1	cup buttermilk
1	teaspoon vanilla extract
1	teaspoon ground cinnamon
1/4	cup lemon juice

In a large bowl, mix flour and salt. Cut in shortening until smooth. Gradually add milk and egg and mix well. On a floured surface, roll dough out very thin. Place in a 10-in. pie pan; set aside.

For filling, cream butter and sugar in a bowl. Add flour. Add eggs, one at a time, beating well after each addition. Stir in remaining ingredients and mix well. Pour into crust.

Bake at 350° for 45 minutes. Cool completely before serving.

perfect pie crust

Here are some quick and easy tips for the perfect pie crust. To enhance the flavor, mix a bit of lemon peel in with the flour. For a firmer crust, add 1/8 teaspoon cream of tartar for each cup of flour. And to cut in shortening quickly and easily into dry ingredients, use a grid-style potato masher.

kentucky chocolate walnut pie

PREP: 15 min. | **BAKE:** 40 min. + cooling | **YIELD:** 6-8 servings.

This is our version of a Southern classic. Crunchy walnuts fill a rich bourbon and chocolate crust. You can use pecans in place of the walnuts if you prefer.

TASTE OF HOME TEST KITCHEN

3	eggs
2	egg yolks
3/4	cup packed brown sugar
2/3	cup light corn syrup
1/3	cup butter, melted
2	tablespoons Kentucky bourbon, optional
1	teaspoon vanilla extract

Dash salt

1	cup coarsely chopped pecans *or* chopped walnuts
1	unbaked pastry shell (9 inches)
1	egg white, lightly beaten
3/4	cup semisweet chocolate chips
1	cup heavy whipping cream
2	tablespoons confectioners' sugar

In a large bowl, whisk the eggs, yolks, brown sugar, corn syrup, butter, bourbon if desired, vanilla and salt. Stir in nuts.

Brush pastry shell with egg white. Sprinkle with chocolate chips. Pour filling over chips. Bake at 350° for 40-45 minutes or until set. Cool on a wire rack.

In a small bowl, beat cream until it begins to thicken. Add confectioners' sugar; beat until stiff peaks form. Dollop on pie just before serving. Refrigerate leftovers.

walnut carrot cake

PREP: 15 min. | **BAKE:** 50 min. + cooling | **YIELD:** 12-16 servings.

This carrot cake is surprisingly moist and flavorful. It also has a great texture with flecks of carrots and walnuts, and it cuts beautifully.

DARLENE BRENDEN, SALEM, OREGON

1	cup butter, softened
1-2/3	cups sugar
4	eggs
1	teaspoon vanilla extract
1	teaspoon grated lemon peel
2-1/2	cups all-purpose flour
1	package (3.4 ounces) instant lemon pudding mix
1-1/2	teaspoons baking powder
1	teaspoon baking soda
1	teaspoon ground cinnamon
1/2	teaspoon salt
1	cup (8 ounces) plain yogurt
2-1/2	cups grated carrots
3/4	cup chopped walnuts
1	can (16 ounces) cream cheese frosting

In a large bowl, cream butter and sugar until light and fluffy. Add eggs, one at a time, beating well after each addition. Beat in the vanilla and lemon peel. Combine the flour, pudding mix, baking powder, baking soda, cinnamon and salt; gradually add to creamed mixture alternately with yogurt, beating well after each addition. Stir in carrots and nuts.

Transfer to a greased and floured 10-in. fluted tube pan. Bake at 350° for 50-55 minutes or until a toothpick inserted near the center comes out clean.

Cool for 10 minutes before removing from pan to a wire rack. Cool completely before frosting. Store in the refrigerator.

walnut carrot cake

caramel-crunch apple pie

caramel-crunch apple pie

PREP: 30 min. | **BAKE:** 40 min. + cooling | **YIELD:** 6-8 servings.

You will be the hit of every party when you bring this sweet pie filled with decadent layers of apples and caramel tucked inside a flaky crust. It's best served warm with a big scoop of ice cream.

BARBARA NOWAKOWSKI, MESA, ARIZONA

28	caramels
2	tablespoons water
5	cups thinly sliced peeled tart apples (about 2 pounds)
1	unbaked pastry shell (9 inches)
3/4	cup all-purpose flour
1/3	cup sugar
1/2	teaspoon ground cinnamon
1/3	cup cold butter, cubed
1/2	cup chopped walnuts

In a heavy saucepan, combine caramels and water. Cook and stir over low heat until melted; stir until smooth.

Arrange a third of the apples in pastry shell; drizzle with a third of the caramel mixture. Repeat layers twice. In a small bowl, combine the flour, sugar and cinnamon; cut in butter until crumbly. Stir in walnuts. Sprinkle over pie.

Bake at 375° for 40-45 minutes or until apples are tender (cover edges with foil during the last 15 minutes to prevent overbrowning if necessary). Cool on a wire rack for 1 hour. Store in the refrigerator.

chopped nuts

If the word "chopped" comes before the ingredient when listed in a recipe, chop the ingredient before measuring. If the word "chopped" comes after the ingredient, chop after measuring.

butterscotch peach pie

PREP: 30 min. + chilling | **BAKE:** 45 min. + cooling
YIELD: 8 servings.

When peach season arrives, this great, old-fashioned pie is sure to be on the table. The recipe has been in our family for over 60 years, and I still make it every summer. Butterscotch buffs will love it.

BARBARA MOYER, TIFFIN, OHIO

2	**cups all-purpose flour**
1	**teaspoon salt**
3/4	**cup shortening**
4	**to 5 tablespoons cold water**

FILLING:

3/4	**cup packed brown sugar**
2	**tablespoons all-purpose flour**
1/3	**cup light corn syrup**
3	**tablespoons butter, melted**
2	**tablespoons lemon juice**
1/4	**teaspoon almond extract**
8	**medium peaches, peeled and sliced**

In a large bowl, combine flour and salt; cut in shortening until crumbly. Gradually add water, tossing with a fork until dough forms a ball. Cover and refrigerate for 30 minutes or until easy to handle.

For filling, in a small saucepan, combine brown sugar and flour. Stir in corn syrup and butter until blended. Bring to a boil; cook and stir for 2 minutes or until thickened. Remove from the heat; stir in lemon juice and extract. Place peaches in a large bowl; add syrup mixture and toss to coat.

Divide dough in half so one ball is slightly larger than the other. Roll out larger ball to fit a 9-in. pie plate. Transfer pastry to plate; trim pastry even with edge. Add filling. Roll out remaining pastry; make a lattice crust. Trim, seal and flute edges. Cover edges loosely with foil.

Bake at 375° for 25 minutes. Uncover; bake 20-25 minutes longer or until crust is golden brown and filling is bubbly. Cool on a wire rack.

lemon-filled coconut cake

PREP: 35 min. | **BAKE:** 25 min. + cooling | **YIELD:** 16 servings.

Around 1970, one of my coworkers brought this cake along with the recipe to a luncheon. It must have made quite an impression on me because I still bake it 40 years later!
JACKIE BERGENHEIER, WICHITA FALLS, TEXAS

1	cup butter, softened
2	cups sugar
3	eggs
2	teaspoons vanilla extract
3-1/4	cups all-purpose flour
3-1/4	teaspoons baking powder
3/4	teaspoon salt
1-1/2	cups 2% milk

FILLING:

1	cup sugar
1/4	cup cornstarch
1	cup water
4	egg yolks, lightly beaten
1/3	cup lemon juice
2	tablespoons butter

FROSTING:

1-1/2	cups sugar
2	egg whites
1/3	cup water
1/4	teaspoon cream of tartar
1	teaspoon vanilla extract
3	cups flaked coconut

In a large bowl, cream butter and sugar until light and fluffy. Add eggs, one at a time, beating well after each addition. Beat in vanilla. Combine the flour, baking powder and salt; add to creamed mixture alternately with milk, beating well after each addition.

Transfer to three greased and floured 9-in. round baking pans. Bake at 350° for 25-30 minutes or until a toothpick inserted near the center comes out clean. Cool for 10 minutes before removing from pans to wire racks to cool completely.

For filling, in a small saucepan, combine sugar, cornstarch and water until smooth. Bring to a boil; cook and stir 2 minutes longer or until thickened and bubbly. Remove from heat.

Stir a small amount of hot mixture into egg yolks; return all to the pan, stirring constantly. Bring to a gentle boil; cook and stir 2 minutes longer. Remove from the heat; gently stir in lemon juice and butter. Cool to room temperature without stirring.

Place one cake on serving plate; spread with half of the filling. Repeat layers. Top with remaining cake.

For frosting, in a large heavy saucepan, combine the sugar, egg whites, water and cream of tartar. With a portable mixer, beat on low speed for 1 minute. Continue beating on low over low heat until frosting reaches 160°, about 10 minutes.

Transfer to a large bowl; add vanilla. Beat on high until stiff peaks form, about 7 minutes. Frost top and sides of cake. Sprinkle with coconut. Store in the refrigerator.

freezer peanut butter pie

PREP: 15 min. + freezing | **YIELD:** 6-8 servings.

If you like peanut butter, you're going to love this pie! It can be made ahead and frozen, so it's perfect for drop-in guests. NINA RUFENER, RITTMAN, OHIO

1	quart vanilla ice cream, softened
1	graham cracker crust (9 inches)
1/2	cup peanut butter
1/3	cup light corn syrup

Chocolate syrup

Chopped walnuts

freezer peanut butter pie

pineapple upside-down cake

In a small bowl, beat egg whites on high speed until stiff peaks form; fold into batter. Spoon into pan.

Bake at 375° for 30-35 minutes or until a toothpick inserted near the center comes out clean. Let stand for 10 minutes before inverting onto serving plate. Place a cherry in the center of each pineapple slice.

PEACH UPSIDE-DOWN CAKE: Omit the pineapple, pecans and cherries. Drain 1 can (15 ounces) sliced peaches, reserving 1/3 cup juice. Arrange peaches over brown sugar. Substitute reserved peach juice for the pineapple juice.

CRANBERRY ORANGE UPSIDE-DOWN CAKE: Omit the pineapple, pecans and cherries. Sprinkle 1 cup halved fresh *or* frozen cranberries and 1 chopped peeled orange over brown sugar. Substitute 1/3 cup orange juice for the pineapple juice.

never-fail pecan pie

PREP: 15 min. | **BAKE:** 45 min. + cooling | **YIELD:** 6-8 servings.

This was my mother-in-law's recipe. Her famous pecan pies were always a hit—you'd never see anyone not enjoy every mouthful! She was kind enough to pass it on to me, and it's one that I use often.
BEVERLY MATERNE, REEVES, LOUISIANA

1/2	cup sugar
1	tablespoon all-purpose flour
1/4	teaspoon salt
2	eggs, well beaten
1	cup dark corn syrup
1	teaspoon vanilla extract
1	cup pecan halves
1	unbaked pastry shell (9 inches)

In a large bowl, combine the sugar, flour, salt, eggs, corn syrup and vanilla. Stir in pecans. Pour into pastry shell. Cover pastry edges with foil to prevent excess browning.

Bake at 350° for 30 minutes. Remove foil and bake another 15 minutes or until golden brown. Cool on a wire rack.

Spread half of the ice cream into crust. Combine peanut butter and corn syrup; spread over ice cream. Top with remaining ice cream. Drizzle with chocolate syrup and sprinkle with nuts.

Cover and freeze for 3-4 hours. Remove from the freezer 15 minutes before serving.

pineapple upside-down cake

PREP: 20 min. | **BAKE:** 30 min. + standing | **YIELD:** 9 servings.

A classic recipe like this never goes out of style. I love it with the traditional pineapple, but peaches or a combination of cranberries and orange also yield good results. BERNARDINE MELTON, PAOLA, KANSAS

1/3	cup butter, melted
2/3	cup packed brown sugar
1	can (20 ounces) sliced pineapple
1/2	cup chopped pecans
3	eggs, *separated*
1	cup sugar
1	teaspoon vanilla extract
1	cup all-purpose flour
1	teaspoon baking powder
1/4	teaspoon salt
9	maraschino cherries

In an ungreased 9-in. square baking pan, combine butter and brown sugar. Drain pineapple, reserving 1/3 cup juice. Arrange 9 pineapple slices in a single layer over sugar (refrigerate any remaining slices for another use). Sprinkle pecans over pineapple; set aside.

In a large bowl, beat egg yolks until thick and lemon-colored. Gradually add sugar, beating well. Blend in vanilla and reserved pineapple juice. Combine the flour, baking powder and salt; add to batter, beating well.

never-fail pecan pie

ozark mountain berry pie

PREP: 15 min. | **BAKE:** 45 min. + cooling | **YIELD:** 8 servings.

I taste the berries or filling before adding to the pie crust to make sure it's sweet enough. Slicing the berries will help them absorb more of the sugar or flavorings. It's delicious served warm.
ELAINE MOODY, CLEVER, MISSOURI

1	**cup sugar**
1/4	**cup cornstarch**
1/2	**teaspoon ground cinnamon, optional**
Dash salt	
1/3	**cup water**
1	**cup fresh blueberries**
Pastry for a double-crust pie (9 inches)	
1	**cup halved fresh strawberries**
1	**cup fresh raspberries**
3/4	**cup fresh blackberries**
1	**tablespoon lemon juice**
2	**tablespoons butter**

In a large saucepan, combine the sugar, cornstarch, cinnamon if desired, salt and water until smooth; add the blueberries. Bring to a boil; cook and stir for 2 minutes or until thickened. Set aside to cool slightly.

Line a 9-in. pie plate with bottom crust; trim pastry even with edge. Gently fold the strawberries, raspberries, blackberries and lemon juice into the blueberry mixture. Pour into pastry; dot with butter. Roll out remaining pastry; make a lattice crust. Trim, seal and flute edges.

Bake at 400° for 10 minutes. Reduce heat to 350°; bake for 45-50 minutes or until the crust is golden brown and filling is bubbly. Cool on a wire rack. Store in the refrigerator.

strawberry rhubarb pie

PREP: 25 min. + chilling | **YIELD:** 8 servings.

My niece tasted this pie at a family dinner and urged me to enter it in our hometown pie contest. She said it would win the Grand Prize, and she was right! I cook at our local nursing home, and everyone enjoys this recipe. JANICE SCHMIDT, BAXTER, IOWA

2	**tablespoons cornstarch**
1	**cup sugar**
1	**cup water**

1	cup sliced rhubarb
3	tablespoons strawberry gelatin powder
1	pastry shell (9 inches), baked
2	pints fresh strawberries, halved

In a large saucepan, mix cornstarch and sugar. Stir in water until smooth. Add rhubarb; cook and stir until clear and thickened. Add gelatin and stir until dissolved. Cool.

Pour about half of rhubarb sauce into pastry shell. Arrange berries over sauce; top with remaining sauce. Refrigerate for 3-4 hours.

blue-ribbon butter cake

PREP: 20 min. | **BAKE:** 65 min. + cooling
YIELD: 12-16 servings.

I found this recipe in an old cookbook I bought at a garage sale. I knew it had been someone's favorite because of the well-worn page...now it's one of mine, too! JOAN GERTZ, PALMETTO, FLORIDA

1	cup butter, softened
2	cups sugar
4	eggs
2	teaspoons vanilla extract
3	cups all-purpose flour
1	teaspoon baking powder
1/2	teaspoon baking soda
1/2	teaspoon salt
1	cup buttermilk

BUTTER SAUCE:

1	cup sugar
1/2	cup butter, cubed
1/4	cup water
1-1/2	teaspoons almond extract
1-1/2	teaspoons vanilla extract

In a large bowl, cream butter and sugar until light and fluffy. Add eggs, one at a time, beating well after each addition. Beat in vanilla. Combine the flour, baking powder, baking soda and salt; add to creamed mixture alternately with buttermilk, beating well after each addition.

Pour into a greased and floured 10-in. tube pan. Bake at 350° for 65-70 minutes or until a toothpick inserted near the center comes out clean. Cool for 10 minutes. Run a knife around edges and center tube of pan. Invert cake onto a wire rack over waxed paper.

For sauce, combine the sugar, butter and water in a small saucepan. Cook over medium heat just until butter is melted and sugar is dissolved. Remove from the heat; stir in extracts.

Poke holes in the top of the warm cake; spoon 1/4 cup sauce over cake. Let stand until sauce is absorbed. Repeat twice. Poke holes into sides of cake; brush remaining sauce over sides. Cool completely.

lemon meringue pie

PREP: 35 min. | **BAKE:** 15 min. + chilling | **YIELD:** 8 servings.

This is my grandmother's recipe for classic lemon meringue pie. It's a special dessert that reminds me of her. MERLE DYCK, ELKFORD, BRITISH COLUMBIA

| 1/2 | cup sugar |
| 1/4 | cup cornstarch |
| Pinch salt |
2	cups cold water
2	egg yolks, lightly beaten
3	tablespoons lemon juice
1	teaspoon grated lemon peel
1	teaspoon butter

MERINGUE:

3	egg whites
1/8	teaspoon cream of tartar
6	tablespoons sugar
Pastry for single-crust pie (9 inches), baked

In a large saucepan, combine the sugar, cornstarch and salt. Stir in water until smooth. Cook and stir over medium heat until thickened and bubbly, about 2 minutes. Reduce heat; cook and stir 2 minutes longer.

Remove from the heat. Gradually stir 1 cup hot filling into egg yolks; return all to the pan. Bring to a gentle boil; cook and stir for 2 minutes. Remove from the heat. Gently stir in lemon juice, peel and butter until butter is melted. Set aside and keep warm.

For meringue, in a small bowl, beat egg whites and cream of tartar on medium speed until soft peaks form. Gradually beat in sugar, 1 tablespoon at a time, on high until stiff glossy peaks form and sugar is dissolved.

Pour filling into crust. Spread meringue over hot filling, sealing edges to crust. Bake at 350° for 15 minutes or until meringue is golden brown. Cool on a wire rack for 1 hour; refrigerate for at least 3 hours before serving.

lemon meringue pie

lemon chess pie

PREP: 15 min. | **BAKE:** 35 min. + chilling | **YIELD:** 6 servings.

This creamy, lemony pie cuts beautifully and has a smooth texture. It simply melts in your mouth.
HANNAH LARUE RIDER, EAST POINT, KENTUCKY

1	sheet refrigerated pie pastry
4	eggs
1-1/2	cups sugar
1/2	cup lemon juice
1/4	cup butter, melted
1	tablespoon cornmeal
2	teaspoons all-purpose flour
1/8	teaspoon salt

Unroll the pastry on a lightly floured surface. Transfer to a 9-in. pie plate. Trim pastry to 1/2 in. beyond edge of plate; flute edges.

In a large bowl, beat eggs for 3 minutes. Gradually add sugar; beat for 2 minutes or until mixture becomes thick and lemon-colored. Beat in the lemon juice, butter, cornmeal, flour and salt.

Pour into the pastry shell. Bake at 350° for 35-40 minutes or until a knife inserted near the center comes out clean. Cool on a wire rack for 1 hour. Refrigerate for at least 3 hours before serving.

lemon chess pie

hummingbird cake

hummingbird cake

PREP: 40 min. | **BAKE:** 25 min. + cooling | **YIELD:** 12-14 servings.

This impressive Southern staple, featuring sweet pinapple flavor and crunchy nuts, is my dad's favorite, so I always make it for his birthday.
NANCY ZIMMERMAN, CAPE MAY COURT HOUSE, NEW JERSEY

2	cups mashed ripe bananas
1-1/2	cups canola oil
3	eggs
1	can (8 ounces) unsweetened crushed pineapple, undrained
1-1/2	teaspoons vanilla extract
3	cups all-purpose flour
2	cups sugar
1	teaspoon salt
1	teaspoon baking soda
1	teaspoon ground cinnamon
1	cup chopped walnuts

PINEAPPLE FROSTING:

1/4	cup shortening
2	tablespoons butter, softened
1	teaspoon grated lemon peel
1/4	teaspoon salt
6	cups confectioners' sugar
1/2	cup unsweetened pineapple juice
2	teaspoons half-and-half cream

Chopped walnuts, optional

In a large bowl, beat the bananas, oil, eggs, pineapple and vanilla until well blended. In another bowl, combine the flour, sugar, salt, baking soda and cinnamon; gradually beat into banana mixture until blended. Stir in walnuts.

Pour into three greased and floured 9-in. round baking pans. Bake at 350° for 25-30 minutes or until a toothpick inserted near the center comes out clean. Cool for 10 minutes before removing from pans to wire racks to cool completely.

For frosting, in a large bowl, beat the shortening, butter, lemon peel and salt until fluffy. Add confectioners' sugar alternately with pineapple juice. Beat in cream. Spread between layers and over top and sides of cake. Sprinkle with walnuts if desired.

texas sheet cake

PREP: 20 min. | **BAKE:** 20 min. + cooling | **YIELD:** 15 servings.

This chocolaty delight was one my mom's specialties. The cake's interior is so moist and the icing glazed on top is so sweet that everyone who samples it always asks for a copy of the recipe.

SUSAN ORMOND, JAMESTOWN, NORTH CAROLINA

1	cup butter, cubed
1	cup water
1/4	cup baking cocoa
2	cups all-purpose flour
2	cups sugar
1	teaspoon baking soda
1/2	teaspoon salt
1/2	cup sour cream

ICING:

1/2	cup butter, cubed
1/4	cup plus 2 tablespoons milk
3	tablespoons baking cocoa
3-3/4	cups confectioners' sugar
1	teaspoon vanilla extract

In a large saucepan, bring the butter, water and cocoa to a boil. Remove from the heat. Combine the flour, sugar, baking soda and salt; add to cocoa mixture. Stir in the sour cream until smooth.

Pour into a greased 15-in. x 10-in. x 1-in. baking pan. Bake at 350° for 20-25 minutes or until a toothpick inserted near the center comes out clean.

In a small saucepan, melt butter; add milk and cocoa. Bring to a boil. Remove from the heat. Whisk in confectioners' sugar and vanilla until smooth. Pour over warm cake. Cool completely on a wire rack.

EDITOR'S NOTE: This recipe does not use eggs.

piece of cake!
Use a pizza cutter to easily cut sheet cakes and brownies. The smooth rolling motion will create clean pieces and none of the bakery will stick to the cutter the way it would on a regular knife.

pound cake ring

PREP: 15 min. | **BAKE:** 1 hour + cooling
YIELD: 2 cakes (9 cups batter).

We've always included pound cake on our family menus. This one has a rich texture that makes it unusually smooth. In addition, the fantastic flavor makes it a special treat each time we serve it.

JOAN PIOTROWSKI, CHICAGO, ILLINOIS

1	pound butter, softened
3	cups sugar
6	eggs
1/2	cup plus 1 tablespoon milk
1	tablespoon lemon juice
1-1/2	teaspoon vanilla extract
1	teaspoon grated lemon peel
1/2	teaspoon lemon extract
4	cups cake flour
1/2	teaspoon salt
1/2	teaspoon baking soda

Confectioners' sugar, fresh peaches, blackberries and mint, optional

In a large bowl, cream butter and sugar until light and fluffy, about 5 minutes. Add eggs, one at a time, beating well after each addition. Combine the milk, lemon juice, vanilla, lemon peel and extract. Combine the flour, salt and baking soda; add to creamed mixture alternately with milk mixture, beating well after each addition.

Pour 4-1/2 cups of batter into a greased and floured 10-in. fluted tube pan. (Use the remaining batter to prepare a second pound cake.)

Bake at 350° for 15 minutes. Reduce heat to 325°; bake 45 minutes longer or until a toothpick inserted near the center comes out clean. Cool for 10 minutes before inverting onto a wire rack to cool completely. Dust with confectioners' sugar and garnish with fruit and mint if desired.

pound cake ring

mardi gras king cake

PREP: 40 min. + rising | **BAKE:** 20 min. + cooling
YIELD: 2 cakes (12 servings each).

This frosted yeast bread is the highlight of our annual Mardi Gras party. It's a festive treat everyone enjoys.
LISA MOUTON, ORLANDO, FLORIDA

- 1 package (1/4 ounce) active dry yeast
- 1/2 cup warm water (110° to 115°)
- 1/2 cup warm milk (110° to 115°)
- 1/3 cup shortening
- 1/3 cup sugar
- 1 teaspoon salt
- 1 egg
- 4 to 4-1/2 cups all-purpose flour
- 2 cans (12-1/2 ounces *each*) almond cake and pastry filling

GLAZE:
- 3 cups confectioners' sugar
- 1/2 teaspoon vanilla extract
- 3 to 4 tablespoons water

Purple, green and gold colored sugar

In a large bowl, dissolve yeast in warm water. Add the milk, shortening, sugar, salt, egg and 2 cups flour. Beat on medium speed for 3 minutes. Beat until smooth. Stir in enough remaining flour to form a soft dough (dough will be sticky).

Turn onto a floured surface; knead until smooth and elastic, about 6-8 minutes. Place in a greased bowl, turning once to grease top. Cover and let rise in a warm place until doubled, about 1 hour.

Punch dough down. Turn onto a lightly floured surface; divide in half. Roll one portion into a 16-in. x 10-in. rectangle. Spread the almond filling to within 1/2 in. of edges. Roll up jelly-roll style, starting with a long side; pinch seam to seal. Place seam side down on a greased baking sheet; pinch ends together to form a ring. Repeat with the remaining dough and filling. Cover and let rise until doubled, about 1 hour.

Bake at 375° for 20-25 minutes or until golden brown. Cool on a wire rack. For glaze, combine the confectioners' sugar, vanilla and enough water to achieve desired consistency. Spread over cooled cakes. Sprinkle with colored sugars.

EDITOR'S NOTE: This recipe was tested with Solo brand cake and pastry filling. Look for it in the baking aisle.

creamy pineapple pie

PREP/TOTAL TIME: 10 min. | **YIELD:** 8 servings.

Here's a light and refreshing dessert that's quick to make and impressive to serve. This is one of our favorite ways to complete a summer meal.
SHARON BICKETT, CHESTER, SOUTH CAROLINA

- 1 can (14 ounces) sweetened condensed milk
- 1 can (8 ounces) crushed pineapple, undrained
- 1/4 cup lemon juice
- 1 carton (8 ounces) frozen whipped topping, thawed
- 1 prepared graham cracker crust (9 inches)

In a large bowl, combine the milk, pineapple and lemon juice. Fold in whipped topping. Pour into prepared crust. Chill until ready to serve.

shoofly pie

PREP: 30 min. | **BAKE:** 45 min. | **YIELD:** 6-8 servings.

We'd melt whenever my grandmother set out this fresh-from-the-oven delight. Shoofly Pie is to the Pennsylvania Dutch what pecan pie is to Southerners.
MARK MORGAN, WATERFORD, WISCONSIN

- 1 unbaked pastry shell (9 inches)
- 1 egg yolk, lightly beaten

FILLING:

- 1/2 cup packed brown sugar
- 1/2 cup molasses
- 1 egg
- 1-1/2 teaspoons all-purpose flour
- 1/2 teaspoon baking soda
- 1 cup boiling water

TOPPING:

- 1-1/2 cups all-purpose flour
- 3/4 cup packed brown sugar
- 3/4 teaspoon baking soda

Dash salt

- 6 tablespoons cold butter

Line pastry with a double thickness of heavy-duty foil. Bake at 350° for 10 minutes. Remove foil; brush crust with egg yolk. Bake 5 minutes longer; cool on a wire rack.

For the filling, in a small bowl, combine the brown sugar, molasses, egg, flour and baking soda; gradually add boiling water. Cool to room temperature; pour the filling into the prepared crust.

For topping, in a large bowl, combine the flour, brown sugar, baking soda and salt. Cut in butter until crumbly. Sprinkle over filling.

Bake at 350° for 45-50 minutes or until golden brown and filling is set. Cool on a wire rack. Store in the refrigerator.

marshmallow-almond key lime pie

PREP: 40 min. | **BAKE:** 15 min. + chilling | **YIELD:** 8 servings.

It's great to see that many grocers now carry key limes, which give this pie its distinctive sweet-tart flavor. JUDY CASTRANOVA, NEW BERN, NORTH CAROLINA

- 1 cup all-purpose flour
- 3 tablespoons brown sugar
- 1 cup slivered almonds, toasted, *divided*
- 1/4 cup butter, melted
- 1 tablespoon honey
- 1 can (14 ounces) sweetened condensed milk
- 1 package (8 ounces) cream cheese, softened, *divided*
- 1/2 cup key lime juice
- 1 tablespoon grated key lime peel

Dash salt

- 1 egg yolk
- 1-3/4 cups miniature marshmallows
- 4-1/2 teaspoons butter
- 1/2 cup heavy whipping cream

Place the flour, brown sugar and 1/2 cup almonds in a food processor. Cover and process until blended. Add melted butter and honey; cover and process until crumbly. Press onto the bottom and up the sides of a greased 9-in. pie plate. Bake at 350° for 8-10 minutes or until crust is lightly browned. Cool on a wire rack.

In a large bowl, beat the milk, 5 ounces cream cheese, lime juice, peel and salt until blended. Add egg yolk; beat on low speed just until combined. Pour into crust. Bake for 15-20 minutes or until center is almost set. Cool on a wire rack.

In a large saucepan, combine the marshmallows and butter. Cook and stir over medium-low heat until melted. Remove from the heat and transfer to a bowl. Add cream and remaining cream cheese; beat until smooth. Cover and refrigerate until chilled.

Beat marshmallow mixture until light and fluffy. Spread over pie; sprinkle with remaining almonds.

marshmallow-almond key lime pie

101

103

104

109

LEMON RICE PUDDING BRULEE

sweet delights

lemon rice pudding brulee

PREP: 30 min. + cooling | **BROIL:** 5 min. | **YIELD:** 6 servings.

Take one sweet bite and you'll fall in love with this tempting rice pudding and creme brulee hybrid. Make the lemonade from frozen concentrate to speed up assembly. HELEN CONWELL, PORTLAND, OREGON

1-1/3	cups lemonade
1/2	cup uncooked long grain rice
1	teaspoon grated lemon peel
1/3	cup plus 3 tablepoons sugar, *divided*
1	tablespoon all-purpose flour
1/2	teaspoon salt
2	cups milk
2	eggs, lightly beaten
1/4	cup dried cranberries
3	tablespoons brown sugar
1/3	cup chopped pecans, toasted

In a small saucepan, bring lemonade and rice to a boil. Reduce heat; cover and simmer for 20 minutes. Remove from the heat; stir in lemon peel. Cover and let stand for 5 minutes. Cool to room temperature.

In a large saucepan, combine 1/3 cup sugar, flour and salt. Stir in milk until smooth. Cook and stir over medium-high heat until thickened and bubbly. Reduce heat; cook and stir 2 minutes longer.

Remove from the heat. Stir a small amount of hot filling into eggs; return all to the pan, stirring constantly. Bring to a gentle boil; cook and stir 2 minutes longer. Remove from the heat. Gently stir in cranberries and cooled rice.

Divide among six 8-oz. ramekins. Place on a baking sheet. Combine brown sugar and remaining sugar. If using a creme brulee torch, sprinkle puddings with sugar mixture. Heat sugar with the torch until caramelized. Sprinkle with pecans. Serve immediately.

If broiling the puddings, place ramekins on a baking sheet; let stand at room temperature for 15 minutes. Sprinkle with sugar mixture. Broil 8 in. from the heat for 4-7 minutes or until sugar is caramelized. Sprinkle with pecans. Serve warm.

easy vanilla ice cream

PREP: 10 min. | **PROCESS:** 20 min. + freezing | **YIELD:** 7 servings.

Three ingredients and an ice cream freezer are all you need for this creamy creation. My husband is diabetic, and this light version fits within his dietary guidelines. JUDY VAHS, MARSHALL, MICHIGAN

2	cups cold fat-free milk
1	can (14 ounces) fat-free sweetened condensed milk
1	package (1 ounce) sugar-free instant vanilla pudding mix

In a large bowl, whisk all ingredients until blended and thickened. Freeze in an ice cream freezer according to the manufacturer's directions.

Transfer to a freezer container. Cover and freeze for 1 hour or until firm.

pinwheel mints

PREP: 45 min. + chilling | **YIELD:** about 3 dozen.

Both my mother and grandmother used to make these eye-catching confections as a replacement for ordinary mints around the holidays. When I offer the treats at parties, guests tell me they taste divine and marvel at the pretty swirl pattern.
MARILOU ROTH, MILFORD, NEBRASKA

1	package (8 ounces) cream cheese, softened
1/2	to 1 teaspoon mint extract
7-1/2	to 8-1/2 cups confectioners' sugar
Red and green food coloring	
Additional confectioners' sugar	

In a large bowl, beat cream cheese and mint extract until smooth. Gradually beat in as much confectioners' sugar as possible; knead in remaining confectioners' sugar until a firm mixture is achieved. Divide mixture in half; with food coloring, tint half pink and the other light green.

On waxed paper, lightly sprinkle remaining confectioners' sugar into a 12-in. x 5-in. rectangle. Divide pink portion in half; shape each portion into a 10-in. log.

Place one log on sugared waxed paper and flatten slightly. Cover with waxed paper; roll into a 12-in. x 5-in. rectangle. Repeat with remaining pink portion; set aside. Repeat with light green portion.

Remove top piece of waxed paper from one pink and one green rectangle. Place one over the other. Roll up jelly-roll style, starting with a long side. Wrap in waxed paper; twist ends. Repeat. Chill overnight.

To serve, cut into 1/2-in. slices. Store in an airtight container in the refrigerator for up to 1 week.

pinwheel mints

1-2-3 blackberry sherbet

PREP: 10 min. + freezing | **YIELD:** 1 quart.

My mom gave me this recipe, which was a favorite when I was young. Now when I make it, my mouth is watering before I'm finished!
LISA EREMIA, IRWIN, PENNSYLVANIA

- 4 **cups fresh *or* frozen blackberries, thawed**
- 2 **cups sugar**
- 2 **cups buttermilk**

In a food processor, combine blackberries and sugar; cover and process until smooth. Strain and discard seeds and pulp. Stir in buttermilk.

Transfer puree to a 13-in. x 9-in. dish. Freeze for 1 hour or until edges begin to firm. Stir and return to freezer. Freeze 2 hours longer or until firm.

Just before serving, transfer to a food processor; cover and process for 2-3 minutes or until smooth.

gingered molasses cookies

PREP: 15 min. | **BAKE:** 10 min./batch | **YIELD:** 5-1/2 dozen.

A nice blend of spices and grated orange peel makes these bites stand out from basic molasses cookies.
DONALD MITCHELL, FREDERICKSBURG, TEXAS

- 1/2 **cup butter, softened**
- 1/4 **cup shortening**
- 1-1/4 **cups sugar, *divided***
- 1 **egg**
- 1/4 **cup molasses**
- 1/2 **teaspoon grated orange peel**
- 2 **cups all-purpose flour**
- 2 **teaspoons baking soda**
- 1/2 **teaspoon salt**
- 1/2 **teaspoon ground ginger**
- 1/2 **teaspoon ground cinnamon**
- 1/4 **teaspoon ground cloves**

In a large bowl, cream the butter, shortening and 1 cup sugar until light and fluffy. Beat in egg, molasses and orange peel. Combine the dry ingredients; gradually add to creamed mixture and mix well.

Roll into 1-1/4-in. balls, then in remaining sugar. Place 2 in. apart on ungreased baking sheets. Bake at 350° for 10-12 minutes or until edges are firm and surface cracks. Remove to wire racks to cool.

punch bowl trifle

PREP: 20 min. | **BAKE:** 20 min. | **YIELD:** 24-28 servings.

I threw together this dessert when I needed something quick to take to my in-laws' house. The luscious layers make it look like you fussed, but it's actually quite easy to make.
KRISTI JUDKINS, MORRISON, TENNESSEE

- 1 **package (18-1/4 ounces) chocolate cake mix**
- 1 **quart fresh whole strawberries**
- 1 **carton (15 ounces) strawberry glaze**
- 2 **cartons (12 ounces each) frozen whipped topping, thawed, *divided***
- 1 **cup chocolate frosting**

Shaved chocolate

Prepare and bake cake according to package directions, using a 13-in. x 9-in. baking pan. Cool completely on a wire rack.

punch bowl trifle

Set aside five strawberries for garnish. Slice remaining strawberries. Cut cake into 1-in. cubes. Place half of the cubes in a 6-qt. glass punch bowl. Top with half of the sliced strawberries; drizzle with half of the strawberry glaze. Spread with 3-1/2 cups whipped topping.

In a microwave-safe bowl, heat frosting on high for 20-30 seconds or until pourable, stirring often; cool slightly. Drizzle half over the whipped topping. Repeat layers of cake, berries, glaze, whipped topping and frosting. Top with remaining whipped topping. Cover and refrigerate until serving. Garnish with shaved chocolate and reserved strawberries.

peach blackberry cobbler

PREP: 40 min. | **BAKE:** 40 min. | **YIELD:** 12 servings.

This is great for a large party or church supper during peach season. You can substitute canned peaches during the off-season, but fresh is always best.
MARGUERITE SHAEFFER, SEWELL, NEW JERSEY

12	medium peaches, peeled and sliced
1/3	cup all-purpose flour
1/4	cup honey
3	tablespoons lemon juice
1/4	teaspoon salt
3	cups fresh blackberries

TOPPING:

2	cups all-purpose flour
1/2	cup sugar
1	teaspoon baking powder
1/2	teaspoon salt
1/4	teaspoon baking soda
1/3	cup cold butter, cubed
1-1/4	cups buttermilk
1	tablespoon coarse sugar

In a large bowl, combine peaches, flour, honey, lemon juice and salt; let stand for 15 minutes. Fold in blackberries. Transfer to a 13-in. x 9-in. baking dish coated with cooking spray.

For topping, in a large bowl, combine the flour, sugar, baking powder, salt and baking soda. Cut in butter until crumbly. Make a well in the center; pour in buttermilk. Stir just until a soft dough forms. Drop by tablespoonfuls over fruit mixture; sprinkle with coarse sugar.

Bake at 400° for 40-45 minutes or until filling is bubbly and a toothpick inserted in topping comes out clean. Serve warm.

caramel pecan shortbread

caramel pecan shortbread

PREP: 30 min. + chilling | **BAKE:** 15 min./batch + cooling
YIELD: about 4 dozen.

My grandchildren look for Grandma's "candy bar cookies" every Christmas. I recommend doubling the recipe for these sweet treats because they go so fast.
DOROTHY BUITER, WORTH, ILLINOIS

3/4	cup butter, softened
3/4	cup confectioners' sugar
2	tablespoons evaporated milk
1	teaspoon vanilla extract
2	cups all-purpose flour
1/4	teaspoon salt

FILLING:

28	caramels
6	tablespoons evaporated milk
2	tablespoons butter
1/2	cup confectioners' sugar
3/4	cup finely chopped pecans

ICING:

1	cup (6 ounces) semisweet chocolate chips
3	tablespoons evaporated milk
2	tablespoons butter
1/2	cup confectioners' sugar
1/2	teaspoon vanilla extract

Pecan halves

In a large bowl, cream butter and confectioners' sugar until light and fluffy. Beat in milk and vanilla. Combine flour and salt; gradually add to creamed mixture. Cover and refrigerate for 1 hour or until easy to handle.

On a lightly floured surface, roll out the dough to 1/4-in. thickness. Cut into 2-in. x 1-in. strips. Place 1 in. apart on greased baking sheets.

Bake at 325° for 12-14 minutes or until lightly browned. Remove to wire racks to cool.

For filling, combine caramels and milk in a large saucepan. Cook and stir over medium-low heat until caramels are melted and smooth. Remove from the heat; stir in the butter, sugar and pecans. Cool for 5 minutes. Spread 1 teaspoon over each cookie.

For icing, in a microwave-safe bowl, melt chips and milk; stir until smooth. Stir in the butter, sugar and vanilla. Cool for 5 minutes.

Spread 1 teaspoon icing on each cookie; top each with a pecan half. Let stand until set. Store in an airtight container.

southern banana pudding

PREP: 30 min. | **BAKE:** 15 min. + chilling | **YIELD:** 8 servings.

This is an old Southern recipe that features a luscious custard layered with bananas and vanilla wafers, then topped with a meringue. It makes a sweet ending to any meal. JAN CAMPBELL, HATTIESBURG, MISSISSIPPI

3/4	cup sugar
1/3	cup all-purpose flour
2	cups 2% milk
2	egg yolks, lightly beaten
1	tablespoon butter
1	teaspoon vanilla extract
36	vanilla wafers
3	medium ripe bananas, cut into 1/4-inch slices

MERINGUE:

2	egg whites
1	teaspoon vanilla extract
1/8	teaspoon cream of tartar
3	tablespoons sugar

In a large saucepan, combine sugar and flour. Stir in milk until smooth. Cook and stir over medium-high heat until thickened and bubbly. Reduce heat; cook and stir 2 minutes longer.

Remove from the heat. Stir a small amount of hot filling into egg yolks; return all to the pan, stirring constantly. Bring to a gentle boil; cook and stir 2 minutes longer. Remove from the heat. Gently stir in butter and vanilla.

In an ungreased 8-in. square baking dish, layer a third of the vanilla wafers, banana slices and filling. Repeat layers twice.

For meringue, in a large bowl, beat the egg whites, vanilla and cream of tartar on medium speed until soft peaks form. Gradually beat in sugar, 1 tablespoon at a time, on high until stiff peaks form. Spread evenly over hot filling, sealing edges to sides of baking dish.

Bake at 350° for 12-15 minutes or until meringue is golden. Cool on a wire rack for 1 hour. Refrigerate for at least 3 hours before serving. Refrigerate leftovers.

peanut butter brownie bars

PREP: 20 min. | **BAKE:** 25 min. + chilling | **YIELD:** 3 dozen.

A brownie mix is the base for this a no-fuss treat that will appeal to adults and children alike. Creamy peanut butter, crunchy nuts and crisp cereal make each bite pure heaven.

RADELLE KNAPPENBERGER, OVIEDO, FLORIDA

1	package fudge brownie mix (13-inch x 9-inch pan size)
12	peanut butter cups, chopped
1/2	cup salted peanuts, chopped
2	cups (12 ounces) semisweet chocolate chips
1-1/4	cups creamy peanut butter
1	tablespoon butter
1-1/2	cups crisp rice cereal
1	teaspoon vanilla extract
1/8	teaspoon salt

Prepare brownie batter according to package directions. Spread into a greased 13-in. x 9-in. baking pan. Bake at 350° for 20-25 minutes or until a toothpick inserted near the center comes out with moist crumbs.

Sprinkle with the peanut butter cups and peanuts. Bake 4-6 minutes longer or until chocolate is melted. Cool on a wire rack.

Meanwhile, in a microwave-save bowl, melt the chocolate chips, peanut butter and butter; stir until smooth. Stir in the cereal, vanilla and salt. Carefully spread over brownies. Cover and refrigerate for at least 2 hours before cutting.

peanut butter brownie bars

buckeyes

buckeyes

PREP: 15 min. + chilling | **YIELD:** about 5-1/2 dozen.

These candies are always popular at my church's annual holiday fund-raiser. For added fun, roll the buckeyes in crisp rice cereal or finely chopped pecans or walnuts while the chocolate is still warm. Then drizzle with melted milk, dark or white chocolate.

MERRY KAY OPITZ, ELKHORN, WISCONSIN

5-1/2	cups confectioners' sugar
1-2/3	cups peanut butter
1	cup butter, melted
4	cups (24 ounces) semisweet chocolate chips
1	teaspoon shortening

In a large bowl, beat the sugar, peanut butter and butter until smooth. Shape into 1-in. balls; set aside.

In a microwave, melt chocolate chips and shortening; stir until smooth. Dip balls in chocolate, allowing excess to drip off. Place on a wire rack over waxed paper; refrigerate for 15 minutes or until firm. Cover and store in the refrigerator.

peanut butter

Before putting peanut butter in a measuring cup, lightly coat the inside with water or oil. The peanut butter slides right out without scraping.

shortbread lemon tart

PREP: 20 min. | **BAKE:** 25 min. + cooling | **YIELD:** 10-12 servings.

For a change of pace from ordinary lemon bars, we added orange peel to both the crust and filling and turned the recipe into a tarts. It's a refreshing finale to a hearty supper. TASTE OF HOME TEST KITCHEN

3	eggs
1/4	cup lemon juice
1-1/4	cups sugar
1	tablespoon grated orange peel
1/4	cup butter, melted

CRUST:

1	cup all-purpose flour
1/3	cup confectioners' sugar
1/2	cup ground almonds
1	teaspoon grated lemon peel
1	teaspoon grated orange peel
1/2	cup cold butter, cubed

Additional confectioners' sugar

For filling, in a blender, combine the eggs, lemon juice, sugar and orange peel. Cover and blend on high until smooth. Add the butter; cover and process on high just until smooth. Set aside.

In a food processor, combine the flour, confectioners' sugar, almonds, lemon peel, orange peel and butter; cover and process until mixture forms a ball. Press pastry onto the bottom and up the sides of an ungreased 9-in. tart pan with removable bottom.

Pour filling into crust. Bake at 350° for 25-30 minutes or until center is almost set. Cool on a wire rack. Just before serving, sprinkle with confectioners' sugar.

shortbread lemon tart

berry shortbread dreams

PREP: 20 min. + chilling | **BAKE:** 15 min.
YIELD: about 3-1/2 dozen.

Raspberry jam adds fruity sweetness to these rich-tasting cookies. They will absolutely melt in your mouth! MILDRED SHERRER, FORT WORTH, TEXAS

1	cup butter, softened
2/3	cup sugar
1/2	teaspoon almond extract
2	cups all-purpose flour
1/3	to 1/2 cup seedless raspberry jam

GLAZE:

1	cup confectioners' sugar
1/2	teaspoon almond extract
2	to 3 teaspoons water

In a large bowl, cream the butter and sugar until light and fluffy. Beat in extract; gradually add flour until dough forms a ball. Cover and refrigerate for 1 hour or until dough is easy to handle.

Roll into 1-in. balls. Place 1 in. apart on ungreased baking sheets. Using the end of a wooden spoon handle, make an indentation in the center. Fill with jam.

Bake at 350° for 14-18 minutes or until edges are lightly browned. Remove to wire racks to cool.

Spoon additional jam into cookies if desired. Combine confectioners' sugar, extract and enough water to achieve drizzling consistency; drizzle over cookies.

grandma's brittle

PREP: 15 min. | **COOK:** 15 min. + cooling
YIELD: about 2-1/2 pounds.

Whenever my grandmother made her famous brittle, every step and ingredient had to be "just right" to guarantee her time-tested results. Watching her make this brittle is one of my favorite memories, and I'm proud to pass on this delicious recipe.
KAREN GRENZOW, SUMAS, WASHINGTON

3	cups sugar
1/2	cup light corn syrup
1	cup water
1/4	cup butter, cubed
1	teaspoon salt
1	jar (16 ounces) unsalted dry roasted peanuts
1-1/2	teaspoons baking soda
1	teaspoon water
1	teaspoon vanilla extract

Grease two baking sheets and keep warm in a 200° oven. In a large saucepan, combine the sugar, corn syrup and 1 cup water. Cook over medium heat, stirring constantly, until a candy thermometer reaches 240° (soft-ball stage). Stir in butter, salt and peanuts. Continue heating, stirring constantly, until the mixture reaches 300°.

Meanwhile, combine the baking soda, 1 teaspoon water and vanilla. Remove saucepan from the heat. Stir in the baking soda mixture. Quickly pour half the mixture over each baking sheet. Spread with a buttered metal spatula to a 1/4-in. thickness. Cool. Break into pieces. Store in an airtight container.

pecan divinity

PREP/TOTAL TIME: 25 min. | **YIELD:** 4 dozen.

The table at our holiday party has a spot reserved for my pecan divinity. I love making candy and have even recruited my husband to help...between nibbles!
CAOLYN WEBER, VICKSBURG, MISSISSIPPI

2	cups sugar
1	cup water
1	jar (7 ounces) marshmallow creme
1	teaspoon vanilla extract
1-1/2	cups chopped pecans

In a large heavy saucepan, combine the sugar and water. Cook over medium heat, without stirring, until a candy thermometer reads 250° (hard-ball stage).

Remove from the heat; stir in the marshmallow creme, vanilla and pecans. Continue stirring until candy cools and begins to hold its shape when dropped from a spoon.

Quickly drop by heaping teaspoonfuls onto a waxed paper-lined baking sheet. Store in an airtight container at room temperature.

EDITOR'S NOTE: We recommend that you test your candy thermometer before each use by bringing water to a boil; the thermometer should read 212°. Adjust your recipe temperature up or down based on your test.

bananas foster

PREP/TOTAL TIME: 25 min. | **YIELD:** 4 servings.

Folks are always impressed when I ignite the rum in this classic Southern dessert.
MARY LOU WAYMAN, SALT LAKE CITY, UTAH

1/3	cup butter, cubed
3/4	cup packed dark brown sugar
1/4	teaspoon ground cinnamon
3	medium bananas
2	tablespoons creme de cacao *or* banana liqueur
1/4	cup dark rum
2	cups vanilla ice cream

In a large skillet or flambe pan, melt butter over medium-low heat. Stir in brown sugar and cinnamon until combined. Cut each banana lengthwise and then widthwise into quarters; add to butter mixture. Cook, stirring gently, for 3-5 minutes or until glazed and slightly softened. Stir in creme de cacao; heat through. Remove from heat.

In a small saucepan, heat rum over low heat until vapors form on surface. Carefully ignite rum and slowly pour over bananas, coating evenly.

Leaving skillet or pan on the cooking surface, gently shake pan back and forth until flames are completely extinguished.

Spoon ice cream into fluted glasses; top with bananas and sauce. Serve immediately.

EDITOR'S NOTE: Keep liquor bottles and other flammables at a safe distance when preparing this dessert. We do not recommend using a nonstick skillet.

bananas foster

ginger fruit crisp

PREP: 20 min. | **BAKE:** 30 min. | **YIELD:** 9 servings.

I've had more than one guest at our bed-and-breakfast tell me that this delectable breakfast crisp starts the day off right. There's seldom a crumb left. ELINOR STABILE, CANMORE, ALBERTA

- 1/3 cup packed brown sugar
- 2 tablespoons plus 1-1/2 teaspoons cornstarch
- 2 cups sliced fresh plums
- 1 cup sliced peeled peaches
- 1 cup sliced nectarines

TOPPING:

- 1 cup crushed gingersnap cookies (about 20 cookies)
- 1/2 cup old-fashioned oats
- 1/3 cup packed brown sugar
- 1/2 teaspoon ground ginger
- 1/2 teaspoon ground cinnamon
- 1/4 teaspoon salt
- 1/3 cup cold butter, cubed
- 1/2 cup sliced almonds

Whipped cream, optional

In a large bowl, combine brown sugar and cornstarch. Add the plums, peaches and nectarines; gently toss to coat. Transfer to a greased 8-in. square baking dish.

For topping, in a small bowl, combine the gingersnap crumbs, oats, brown sugar, ginger, cinnamon and salt. Cut in butter until crumbly. Stir in almonds; sprinkle over fruit.

Bake at 350° for 30-35 minutes or until the filling is bubbly and topping is browned. Serve warm with whipped cream if desired.

ginger fruit crisp

new orleans bread pudding

new orleans bread pudding

PREP: 35 min. | **BAKE:** 35 min. | **YIELD:** 12 servings.

Try this sweet and buttery bread pudding for a taste of the Big Easy. We live out west and serve it to the cowboys at our ranch. LINDA WIESE, PAYETTE, IDAHO

- 1/2 cup raisins
- 1/4 cup brandy *or* unsweetened apple juice
- 1/2 cup butter, melted, *divided*
- 1 tablespoon sugar
- 4 eggs, lightly beaten
- 2 cups half-and-half cream
- 1 cup packed brown sugar
- 2 teaspoons vanilla extract
- 1/2 teaspoon salt
- 1/2 teaspoon freshly ground nutmeg
- 10 slices day-old French bread (1 inch thick), cubed

SAUCE:

- 1/2 cup packed brown sugar
- 2 tablespoons cornstarch

Dash salt

- 1 cup cold water
- 1 tablespoon butter
- 2 teaspoons vanilla extract

In a small saucepan, combine raisins and brandy. Bring to a boil. Remove from heat; cover and set aside. Brush a shallow 2-1/2-qt. baking dish with 1 tablespoon butter; sprinkle with sugar and set aside.

In a large bowl, combine the eggs, cream, brown sugar, vanilla, salt and nutmeg. Stir in remaining butter and reserved raisin mixture. Gently stir in bread; let stand for 15 minutes or until bread is softened.

Transfer to prepared dish. Bake, uncovered, at 350° for 35-40 minutes or until a knife inserted near center comes out clean.

For sauce, in a small saucepan, combine the brown sugar, cornstarch and salt; gradually add water. Bring to a boil; cook and stir for 1-2 minutes or until thickened. Remove from the heat; stir in butter and vanilla. Serve with bread pudding.

macadamia fudge

PREP: 20 min. + chilling | **YIELD:** about 2 pounds.

There are few recipes I just have to pull out every holiday season, and this fudge is one of them. It couldn't be easier or more indulgent!

TINA JACOBS, WANTAGE, NEW JERSEY

1-1/2	teaspoons butter, softened
3	cups (18 ounces) semisweet chocolate chips
1	can (14 ounces) sweetened condensed milk
Pinch salt	
1	cup chopped macadamia nuts
1-1/2	teaspoons vanilla extract

Line an 8-in. square pan with foil and grease the foil with butter; set aside.

In a heavy saucepan, combine the chocolate chips, milk and salt. Cook and stir over low heat until chips are melted. Remove from the heat; stir in nuts and vanilla. Pour into prepared pan. Chill for 2 hours or until firm.

Using foil, lift fudge out of pan. Gently peel off foil; cut fudge into 1-in. squares.

bourbon balls

PREP: 30 min. + chilling | **YIELD:** 4 dozen.

Dark chocolate and chopped pecans flavor these simple, spirited treats. Make a double batch so you can give some as gifts and savor the rest yourself!

TASTE OF HOME TEST KITCHEN

1-1/4	cups finely chopped pecans, *divided*
1/4	cup bourbon
1/2	cup butter, softened
3-3/4	cups confectioners' sugar
1	pound dark chocolate candy coating, melted

Combine 1 cup pecans and bourbon; cover and let stand for 8 hours or overnight.

In a large bowl, cream butter and confectioners' sugar until light and fluffy; stir in pecan mixture. Cover and refrigerate for 45 minutes or until firm enough to shape into 1-in. balls. Place on waxed paper-lined baking sheets. Chill for 1 hour or until firm.

Dip in chocolate coating; allow excess to drip off. Sprinkle with remaining pecans. Let stand until set.

pecan caramels

PREP: 20 min. | **COOK:** 35 min. + cooling
YIELD: about 2-1/2 pounds.

I altered the original recipe for these creamy caramels by substituting condensed milk for part of the whipping cream and cutting back on the sugar. Everybody raves about them, and they make a great holiday gift. You can't eat just one!
PATSY HOWELL, PERU, INDIANA

1	tablespoon butter, softened
1	cup sugar
1	cup light corn syrup
2	cups heavy whipping cream, *divided*
1	can (14 ounces) sweetened condensed milk
2	cups chopped pecans
1	teaspoon vanilla extract

Line a 13-in. x 9-in. pan with foil; grease the foil with butter. Set aside.

In a large heavy saucepan, combine the sugar, corn syrup and 1 cup cream. Bring to a boil over medium heat. Cook and stir until smooth and blended, about 10 minutes. Stir in milk and remaining cream. Bring to a boil over medium-low heat, stirring constantly. Cook and stir until a candy thermometer reads 238° (soft-ball stage), about 25 minutes.

Remove from the heat; stir in pecans and vanilla. Pour into prepared pan (do not scrape saucepan). Cool. Using foil, lift candy out of pan; cut into 1-in. squares. Wrap individually in waxed paper.

EDITOR'S NOTE: We recommend that you test your candy thermometer before each use by bringing water to a boil; the thermometer should read 212°. Adjust your recipe temperature up or down based on your test.

caramel crystals

The recipe for Pecan Caramels advises against scraping the pan to prevent the candy syrup from forming crystals or becoming grainy. There is a difference in the crystallization of the candy mixture that is nearer the top of the pan and that which is near the bottom of the pan, which is exposed to greater heat.

tea cakes

PREP: 10 min. | **BAKE:** 10 min./batch | **YIELD:** 9 dozen.

I've baked many batches of different cookies throughout the years, but my friends and family tell me these are the best. The simple butter flavor just melts in your mouth.

DORIS MCGOUGH, DOTHAN, ALABAMA

1	**cup butter, softened**
1-1/2	**cups sugar**
3	**eggs**
1	**tablespoon vanilla extract**
3	**cups all-purpose flour**
1	**tablespoon baking powder**
1/4	**teaspoon salt**

In a large bowl, cream the butter and sugar until light and fluffy. Add eggs, one at a time, beating well after each addition. Beat in vanilla. Combine the flour, baking powder and salt; gradually add to the creamed mixture (the dough will be soft).

Drop by teaspoonfuls 2 in. apart onto greased baking sheets. Bake at 375° for 7-8 minutes or until the edges are golden brown. Remove to wire racks to cool.

southern-style soft custard

PREP/TOTAL TIME: 30 min. | **YIELD:** 8 servings.

This recipe has been handed down in my family through many generations. Custard is one of our favorite desserts for holidays and special occasions. I also take this indulgent treat to neighbors and friends when they are feeling under the weather because the smooth texture soothes sore throats.

MARGARET ALLEN, ABINGDON, VIRGINIA

3	**egg yolks**
1/4	**cup sugar**
1/8	**teaspoon salt**
2	**cups whole milk**
1/2	**teaspoon vanilla extract**

Sliced pound cake

Fresh berries of choice

Beat together egg yolks, sugar and salt. Scald milk (heat to 180°) and pour slowly over egg mixture. Place mixture in top of double boiler and cook over simmering (not boiling) water; stir constantly until mixture reaches 160° or is thick enough to coat the back of a spoon.

Mixture will not have the consistency of a firm baked custard. Cool over ice water, stirring occasionally. Add the vanilla. If the mixture separates, beat with egg beater until smooth. Serve custard chilled over sliced pound cake; top with berries of your choice.

bourbon pecan pralines

bourbon pecan pralines

PREP: 15 min. | **COOK:** 25 min. + standing | **YIELD:** 1 pound.

Just like authentic pralines found in New Orleans, these pop-in-your-mouth treats are sweet, crunchy and rich! TASTE OF HOME TEST KITCHEN

1/4	**cup butter, cubed**
1/2	**cup sugar**
1/2	**cup packed brown sugar**
3/4	**cup heavy whipping cream**
1	**cup pecan halves, toasted**
1/2	**cup chopped pecans, toasted**
1	**tablespoon bourbon**

Grease two baking sheets; set aside. In a large heavy saucepan over medium heat, melt butter. Stir in the sugars, then cream; cook and stir until mixture comes to a boil. Cook, stirring occasionally, until a candy thermometer reads 236° (soft-ball stage), about 20 minutes.

Remove from the heat; stir in the pecan halves, chopped pecans and bourbon. Immediately drop by tablespoonfuls onto prepared baking sheets. Let stand until pralines are set and no longer glossy. Store in an airtight container.

EDITOR'S NOTE: We recommend that you test your candy thermometer before each use by bringing water to a boil; the thermometer should read 212°. Adjust your recipe temperature up or down based on your test.

general recipe index

This index lists every recipe by food category and/or major ingredient, so you can easily locate recipes that suit your needs.

alphabetical index

This index lists every recipe in alphabetical order so you can easily find your favorite recipes.